GET OFF MY BRAIN

A Survival Guide for Lazy* Students

*Bored, Frustrated, and Otherwise Sick of School

Randall McCutcheon

Foreword by Steve Allen
Illustrations by Pete Wagner

D0012266

free spirit
PUBLiSHiNG®

Works
for kids®

Library of Congress Cataloging in Publication Data

McCutcheon, Randall, 1949–
    Get off my brain : a survival guide for lazy students / Randall McCutcheon ; foreword by Steve Allen ; illustrations by Pete Wagner.
    — Rev. ed.
       p. cm.
    Includes index.
    ISBN 1-57542-037-6
    1. Study skills. 2. Underachievers. I. Wagner, Pete. II. Title.
LB1049.M33 1998
371.3'028'1—dc21   97-39354
                                                                              CIP
                                                                               AC

At the time of this book's publication, all facts and figures cited are the most current available; all telephone numbers, addresses, and Web site URLs are accurate and active; all publications, organizations, Web sites, and other resources exist as described in this book; and all have been verified. The author and Free Spirit Publishing make no warranty or guarantee concerning the information and materials given out by organizations or content found at Web sites, and we are not responsible for any changes that occur after this book's publication. If you find an error or believe that a resource listed here is not as described, please contact Free Spirit Publishing. Parents, teachers, and other adults: We strongly urge you to monitor children's use of the Internet.

Credits
Summary of Learning Styles information, pages 18–23, reprinted by permission. Copyright © 1995, 1996 by Kathleen A. Butler, Ph.D., author of *Viewpoints: A Prelude to Learning Styles*. Published by the Learner's Dimension. Excerpt on page 74 from *The Book of Lists* #2 by Irving Wallace, David Wallechinsky, Amy Wallace, and Sylvia Wallace. Copyright © 1980 by Irving Wallace, David Wallechinsky, Amy Wallace, and Sylvia Wallace. By permission of William Morrow & Company. Illustration on page 92 reprinted by permission of the artist, J. C. Duffy. Copyright © 1981 Kersten Bros. Co. Summary from *Just in Time*, pages 92–93, used with permission of the author, Robert D. Rutherford. Copyright © 1981 by Robert Rutherford. Published by Keneric Publishing Company.

Interior design by Julie Odland Smith
Index compiled by Eileen Quam

10 9 8 7 6 5 4
Printed in the United States of America

Free Spirit Publishing Inc.
217 Fifth Avenue North, Suite 200
Minneapolis, MN 55401-1299
(612) 338-2068
help4kids@freespirit.com
www.freespirit.com

The following are registered trademarks of Free Spirit Publishing Inc.:
FREE SPIRIT®
FREE SPIRIT PUBLISHING®
SELF-HELP FOR TEENS®
SELF-HELP FOR KIDS®
WORKS FOR KIDS®
THE FREE SPIRITED CLASSROOM®

For my grandmother

Acknowledgments

Special thanks to these student contributors:

Jessica Bankston
Preeta Bansal
Brian Chaffin
Val Gaddis
Amy Garwood
Cara Hansen
Jessica Hass
Laura Hochia
Tonja Holder
Ladan Jafari
Katie Johnson
Reah Johnson
Jonah Klevesahl
Tom Lyon
Sue Lyon
John Nielson
Craig Smith
Julie Uribe
John Vitek
Jason Wesbecher

Contents

Foreword by Steve Allen vii

Why School Can Be Deadly 1
    What Lazy Means   2
    The Getting-Bored Address   7

Surviving the Same Old Same Old 9
    The Meaningless Question   9
    Fili-blustering   11
    The Fake Argument   11
    Leave Skipping to Lou   12
    Sit in the Front Row   13

Know Thyself 16
    Learning Styles   16

Nobody "Brown-Nosed" the Trouble I've Seen 24
    Five Pointers to Living Apple-y Ever After   24
    Teachers Are People, Too   27

All Work and No Wordplay 34
    The Empty Bucket Theory   35
    Variations on a Theme   35
    Parodies   36
    Letters to the Editor   38

The Thrill of the Hunt 41
    Fact Finding   42
    Unweaving the Tangled Web   45

New Kid on the Writer's Block 48
    Never Lose Interest in Borrowing   50
    Literary Lessons   53
    Paper Train Yourself   56

You Can Have Your Cake and Edit, Too 67

Ver-bull-izing 73
    Suggestions for the Scared Speechless   75

This Is Only a Test 79

Cutting Costs the McCutcheon Way 89

Time Rarely Flies 91

Index 98

About the Author 101

FOREWORD

BY STEVE ALLEN,
AUTHOR AND ENTERTAINER

George Bernard Shaw's observation that it's a great pity youth is wasted on the young can certainly be applied to the process by which most of us become formally educated. Schooling seems to come at the most inopportune time, at least for many of us. Unless we have the good fortune to be addicted to reading, to thirst after knowledge for its own sake, or to be fascinated by a given subject, it is quite possible for us to complete four or more years at an institution of higher learning and yet remain remarkably ignorant.

Part of the reason is that just at the time we are supposed to become scholars we suffer the distraction of having to learn to become adults. We are, understandably, preoccupied with the opposite sex, the tiresome but quite necessary burden of soon earning a living, the uncomfortable sensation of for the first time having our prejudices called into question, not to mention the thousand-and-one diversions that American life forces upon us by means of television, radio, popular music, videos, cell phones, pagers, the Internet, newspapers and magazines of dubious gravity, sports, election campaigns that insult our intelligence, crimes, and assorted trivia.

Small wonder, then, that what is supposed to be true education is, for millions, a sort of comedy of errors.

To refer to only one example:

A recent Gallup poll points to the incredible ignorance of U.S. citizens concerning matters of simple geography. The results showed that one adult American in seven couldn't locate the U.S. on an unmarked world map! One in four couldn't find the Pacific Ocean. Younger adults, those ages 18–24, scored even worse. They came in last in a geography survey compared to young adults in most of Western Europe, Canada, Japan, and Mexico.

Reports like these are all too typical. Mountains of evidence—in the form of both statistical studies and personal testimonies—establish that the American people are suffering from a new and perhaps unprecedented form of mental incapacitation for which I have coined the word "dumbth."

Well, if things are this bad—and only because of limitations of space is it impossible to establish here that they are far worse—then almost any constructively remedial weapon, including that of humor, ought to be resorted to, and fast.

A too-hasty reading of Mr. McCutcheon's argument might suggest that he is really giving tips on how to sneak by, pass tests with a minimum of study, or graduate with the least expenditure of energy. Not so; the author is obviously as interested as any other dedicated educator in producing students who have at least approached the limits of their potential. His playful, jocular approach will certainly interest students who would have reacted negatively to a more traditional approach. The few natural geniuses do not especially require McCutcheon's assistance. The few dolts are unlikely to profit by it.

But there are undoubtedly many others who will respond favorably to this tongue-in-cheek book, with its winning combination of wit and wisdom.

Why School Can Be Deadly

"Education [is] not as sudden as a massacre
but [it is] more deadly in the long run."

Mark Twain

My grandfather used to say, "Yep . . . I went through school . . ." (a somewhat overly melodramatic pause) ". . . in the front door and out the back."

Since then I have heard too many students express the same sentiment. And they weren't joking.

During interviews with students about their school experiences, the following sentiments kept being repeated:

"School is such a waste of time." Jon, 17

"Teachers and classes don't require students to think." Kevin, 18

"I get so bored in class that any motivation I had to begin with is soon lost. Then I don't want to do anything in school." Devon, 18

1

> **"I'm tired of being held back in school. In fact, I'm just tired."** Regina, 15

School can be deadly to your scholarly life—you may be left feeling bored, unmotivated, and just plain tired. Unfortunately for most of us, the resources that are available to ease the scholarly life of the lazy student are sadly lacking. It is true that bookstore reference shelves are lined with study guides, but they invariably make the same false assumptions:

- ◎ Students can study for several hours every night and still maintain their sanity.

- ◎ All students set specific long-range goals and follow through with action.

- ◎ Research abilities are innate.

- ◎ All classes are equally interesting.

- ◎ Students are never incapacitated by personal crises, let alone adolescent mooncalfing or lollydolling.*

- ◎ Students are willing to read hundreds of humorless pages written in tiresome prose to discover that being a "good" student is nearly impossible for a normal person.

This book is nothing more than a simple attempt to change the course of academic history. And it is written for you . . . the normal, bright, lazy student.

But just exactly what is *"lazy"*?

What Lazy Means

According to psychologist Dr. Thomas Greenspon of Minneapolis, Minnesota, words like *lazy* may be descriptors for "those who choose not to do what we (teachers and parents, or society at large) think they should be doing."

---

* June Cleaver's words to describe Wally's first experience in wooing.

2

The reasons for this unwillingness to conform (and perform) are numerous. For example:

1. Some people are such perfectionists that everything must be just right in order for them to feel successful.

> **"I always think, 'I'm so intelligent, therefore I should get A's no matter what the subject is.'"** Missy, 17

People who do things in order to live up to the expectations of others, or who set unreasonably high goals for themselves, often simply stop trying. They become "lazy" so they no longer have to worry about not being perfect. If this sounds like you, ease up on yourself. Note these words from a reformed perfectionist:

> **"It was when I stopped trying to do everything right that I started doing things well."** Jana, 15

2. Students who breeze through the elementary school days may suffer from a lack of study skills when they reach more challenging classes. Simply showing up to class won't be enough anymore.

If you find yourself in this situation, don't give in to the temptation to simply zone out and use the excuse "I never learned how to do this, so what's the point in trying now?" Clichéd as it may be: It's never too late to learn.

3. Students discouraged by a few bad grades or dull classes begin to think that their days in school are an abysmal waste of time. You might find that your brand of lazy stems from feeling bored, frustrated, and otherwise sick of school. Perhaps you've already mastered the subject matter being presented. Maybe your instructors were not blessed with a personality. Whatever the case, don't despair. There is still hope for you.

Finally, if you are lazy, remember that you are not alone:

"Lazy means always being depressed because you never get anything accomplished." Jenessa, 17

"It is my favorite way of saying no!" Mikal, 15

"Lazy: (in-tel-ij-ent): (origin obscure, probably from Latin G. *Lazius Efortulus,* the only Roman who did not leave a twenty-volume collection of memoirs to plague future generations . . . best known for his famous query 'So what?' *Adj.* **1:** the condition or state of cleverness **2:** the extraordinary ability to meet life head down **3:** having sufficient willpower and stamina to avoid mundane drudgery while at the same time harvesting the fruits of mental inactivity (See also 'coma')." **Brian, 17**

'SO WHAT?'

With tongue in cheek and, most likely, head on pillow, these students have suggested the purpose of this book: To help you survive in school. And if the principles outlined in this guide are applied consistently and creatively, you will not only survive; you will thrive.

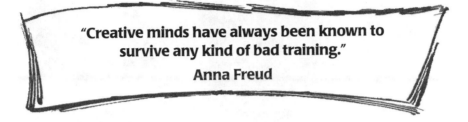

"Creative minds have always been known to survive any kind of bad training."
Anna Freud

In the pages that follow, you will learn strategies that will make you more effective in the classroom—everything from how to amuse yourself in boring classes to how to improve your grade point average with less effort. And, more importantly, how to actually learn something in school.

These strategies will work for you unless the symptoms of your laziness are related to more serious problems than those previously outlined. For example, if you have a *debilitating* fear of failure, a learning difference or physical disability that hasn't been appropriately dealt with, or absolutely no support systems, the help you need demands more attention than this book can provide. Such obstacles need to be confronted with the help of trained professionals. If you suspect you need specialized assistance, RUN to the nearest counselor, psychologist, family physician, special education teacher, or other trusted adult. Explain your concerns and get help in deciding what action should be taken.

For those of you who are just normally lazy, begin now. Prepare yourself for the wonderful world of rest and relaxation awarded to students willing to learn to play the system.

"Somebody's boring me ... I think it's me."
Dylan Thomas

The Getting-Bored Address

(With my apologies to one of our tallest presidents)

Nobody kept score and many cheers ago, our poor teachers brought forth the concept, conceived in mediocrity, that all students are created equal and therefore need only be equally creative.

Now we are engaged in a back-to-basics bedlam. We have made our bedlam, but it is the students who must lie in it. Therefore, it is altogether fitting and proper that we should stop lying.

But in a larger sense we can no longer demonstrate, we can no longer educate, we can no longer create in the classroom. The brave minds, dead and dying, who struggle there, may never create but they can add and subtract.

True, the world will little note nor long remember what we say here, but generations of students will be forced to memorize it verbatim and pass a true-false test. And so it is rather for us, the thinking, to abhor the dead minds and spreading behinds with our last full measure of revulsion: That we here highly resolve that there must be a new birth of free thinking, and that the creativity of the students, by the students, and for the students shall not perish from education.

If Abraham Lincoln had been a young man today, forced to sit through semester after semester of middle school, high school, or college classes, he probably would have remained a railsplitter.

Yes, friends, the uncivil war between teachers and students rages on. And emancipation is a futile flight of fancy, so you might as well begin preparing for battle.

Surviving the Same Old Same Old

I believe there are strategies you can employ to survive even the deadliest of doldrums. To paraphrase Thoreau: You must learn to march to the beat of a different doldrummer. Try experimenting with these activities to fill those times when the teacher is unable, or you are unwilling, to fill your mind.

The Meaningless Question

This strategy involves getting the teacher sidetracked into discussing an irrelevant subject so that you can allow your mind to wander freely.

Two keys to success:

1. Make sure your question generates an answer that will not include testable material or you lose the game, and

2. Carefully monitor the mood of the teacher so that your plan does not cause the teacher to become angry with you.

Here are some examples of "meaningless" questions:

⑨ "I've always wondered, how does school differ today from when you were a student?"*

⑨ "Since teachers are professionals—just like doctors and lawyers—why aren't they paid more money?"

⑨ "In Shakespeare's play, Hamlet is confronted with the choice of 'to be or not to be.' When you were growing up, were you ever depressed enough to seriously consider suicide?"

(Please note, it is a safe bet that most teachers and professors have been seriously depressed—that seems to be a prerequisite for the job. And remember that this question can be adapted to almost any poem, short story, or novel. Fortunately for you, most writers are always depressed, too.)

* This type of question is best used before a serious discussion starts or near the end of the period when it is obvious that even the teacher is bored.
** The beauty of this question is that it works for any subject. Simply delete "Math" and plug in the other possibilities.

Fili-blustering

This strategy and the next one require a willingness to speak, at length, in class. (Turn to pages 73–78 for suggestions on passing your "orals.") The trick is to pick an issue that is being discussed and see how long you can talk without being interrupted by another student or the teacher. Keep track of your progress, recording your times and an evaluation of your fluency in a special notebook.

Again, be warned that this works best when the mood is right. It is interesting to note, however, how many teachers appear grateful not to have to teach. Proceed with caution.

The Fake Argument

This strategy requires being in cahoots with a fellow classmate. All you do is wait for a controversial issue to be discussed in class. Immediately one of you should make a strong statement defending a position (e.g., on the subject of capital punishment).

◎ "Anyone who commits an intentional felony should be shot!"

Then the other, just as quickly, contradicts the thesis of the first position:

◎ "Anyone who would make a ridiculous statement like that should be shot!"

The argument continues from there until someone interrupts you, at which time you record in your notebook the results of your latest effort.

As before, the same precautions apply. In addition, you should be careful not to let the logic of your arguments, or the intense passion with which you present them, offend the teacher's sensibilities.

Leave Skipping to Lou

Clearly, you cannot experiment with the aforementioned activities unless you attend class. You cannot learn, either. So if amusing yourself with these strategies is not enough incentive to get you to class, then consider the following independent reasons:

◎ The teacher's ego can be your downfall. Many teachers have gone on to achieve M.A. and Ph.D. degrees. That takes sacrifice. When you skip class, some teachers take that to mean you are questioning the importance of their work. It is an insult to them. It is rejection. In short, they won't like you. Often they will find a way to punish you. Lower grades, for example.

> **"Coming to class is essential. As soon as the teacher becomes aware of how much you care, you will be subject to the same treatment the other students have been receiving all along."** Josh, 15

> **"Some students are careful not to answer too many questions in class so others won't think them 'teacher's pet' or 'goody-goody.' But I have to admit that participating a lot in class helps to alleviate boredom. Besides, students don't give out the grades."** Mara, 18

◎ Many teachers test out of their notes. There is a correlation between a teacher's subject intelligence level and the need to study lecture notes. In other words, the more the teacher knows, the less likely there is a need to rely on the textbook to create questions for the test. With a little research and an educated guess, you can determine where to allocate your limited study time. Sometimes you may not need to read the textbook at all. (For more tips on test taking, see pages 79–88.)

- You will understand the notes better if you take them. The classic rationalization, "Oh, I don't need to go to class today, I'll just borrow Johnny's notes," demonstrates how naive you are about the process of understanding both complex explanations and Johnny.

- Your attendance and careful note-taking decrease the need for outside study. Normally, borrowed notes or a short recapitulation in study hall or back at the dorm do not give a clear assessment of what material was most important to learn. The teacher, through nonverbal clues and various asides (e.g., "That Freudian application I just explained for the last 20 minutes is just for your own edification and will not be on the test!"), suggests areas on which to focus your study efforts. Do your friends write down these clues and asides? Don't make me laugh.

Sit in the Front Row

There is no reason to cheat off the student sitting next to you when you can tap his or her talents through the legitimate use of logistics. In other words, put up a good front by sitting up front.

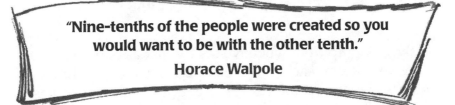

> **"Nine-tenths of the people were created so you would want to be with the other tenth."**
>
> **Horace Walpole**

You will often meet brighter, even more ambitious students than yourself by sitting in the front row. It is true that the academically gifted are likely to plop down anywhere; but a higher percentage, row-wise, will be near the teacher. If you're in college, you'll note that graduate students inevitably gravitate in that direction. Make friends with these people, play up to them, pat their heads, give them your full attention.

What does this mean for you? These front-row students are more likely to take good notes that you can borrow if you absolutely must miss class (reread pages 12–13). If you don't understand some of the lecture material and the teacher is usually busy after class, these students are the next best thing. Plus, they will be able to provide superior insight when trying to second-guess potential test questions.

You are less likely to fall asleep when sitting in the front row. Snoring is visible, noisy, and embarrassing. So is drooling on your desk.

A "BELL CURVE" SEATING CHART

By sitting up front, you give the teacher a chance to get to know you. If the teacher is at all approachable, you have, as they say, headed off the other students at the pass (and passing, after all, is the name of the game). Clearly, if the teacher is prone to fits of gabbiness, then it is a simple matter to introduce yourself, and at the same time, remove yourself from the stigma of being just another face in the crowd.

It is a good idea to choose your position in the front row next to a student you are certain the teacher likes. Remember the childhood advice not to sit too close to the fire (i.e., naughty students) or you would get burned? Well, a corollary is true: Sit by likable, bright students and you will get en-light-ened.

When you sit in the front row, your confidence level will increase. Besides the obvious merits of no guilt trip for skipping out or falling asleep, it is likely you will feel more positive when studying for exams if you have attended and listened. A positive attitude can be critical in passing the threshold of trying, and thus, in passing the class.

Random Thoughts

At some point(s) in your career as a student, emotional trauma will interfere with your desire to attend class, perhaps even with your desire to move. You will begin to question the meaning of life and the need to be responsible. You will sleep too much, too little, or not at all. For many students this is when the G.P.A. (grade poop average) hits the fan.

Ah, sweet romantics, lazy learners, fellow passengers on that ship of foolish behavior: Your ship, your future, is sinking.

**"Never despair, but if you do,
work on in despair."
Edmund Burke**

Go to class . . . do not pass go. Go! Go! Go! If you don't, you may not end up in jail, but you won't end up owning your own monopoly either.

KNOW THYSELF

In selecting classes, whenever possible, choose by teacher—not by course. Try to match your personality and learning style with the personality and teaching style of each prospective teacher.

> **"Socrates once advised to 'know thyself' which explains why he was the teacher."** Amy, 17

For example, it makes little sense to choose a teacher who gives only essay questions if your preference is for the objective test. Nor does it make sense to sign up with a boring lecturer if the same class is taught by "Mr. Movie" with his video collection that rivals Blockbuster.

Learning Styles

The unique and highly individualized way in which you learn is your *learning style*. Some students learn best by *listening* (lectures, tapes); others learn best by *seeing* (reading books, the board, charts, graphs). Still others learn best by *touching* and *moving* (building models, using hands-on materials, solving puzzles).

Some students are explorers who view a question or problem from many different angles before arriving at an answer.

Others make decisions quickly. Some students are down-to-earth; others are dreamers. Some are highly organized; some prefer a perpetual state of chaos. There are the risk-takers and the play-it-safers. There are the students who learn best in groups, and those who are loners. The list of learning styles goes on and on.

The more you know about your learning style, the more you can take advantage of your learning strengths. To learn more about it, spend time doing a bit of research and self-assessment. A few hours of pre-semester soul searching, interviews with former students, and the completion of personality "Prof"-iles (see pages 27–33) can save weeks of torture, tongue-biting, and tedium. The concept is well-researched and worth exploring, but don't take my word for it. Here's what students who have studied learning styles have to say about it:

> **"Studying learning styles helped me understand why some teachers (who don't teach to my style) frustrate me."** Natalie, 17

> **"Knowing about learning styles helps me to transcend difficult situations and difficult people."** Mark, 16

> **"Now I finally have an excuse for starting my homework at 10:00 on a Sunday night."** Sara, 17

> **"It helped me realize how well-rounded I really am."** Jade, 15

In her book *Viewpoints*, learning styles expert Kathleen Butler discusses five major learning style types. All of us have some of the features of each style, yet most people exhibit dominant characteristics from one of these categories. The pages that follow provide an abbreviated look at Butler's discussion of learning styles.

Realistic

Core Qualities as Thinkers

- Information-based
- Interested in production
- Objective, ask how
- To-the-point with detail
- Reliable, tenacious

Behavior with Others

- Respect authority
- Like to be in control
- Want guided practice
- Straightforward, responsible

Needs as Learners

- Crisp, linear directions
- Specific assignments
- Charts, data, tools
- Orderly surroundings
- Practical applications
- Structured, graphic methods: timelines, graphs, models

Analytical

Core Qualities as Thinkers

⇨ Logical, conceptual

⇨ Knowledge-oriented

⇨ Skeptical, ask why

⇨ Focused on goals, the long term

⇨ Examining, critical

Behavior with Others

⇨ Driven by achievement

⇨ Like intellectual recognition

⇨ Debate with others

⇨ Like to work alone

Needs as Learners

⇨ Intellectual dialogue

⇨ Research topics, theories

⇨ Books, references

⇨ Space to work alone

⇨ Ideas, teacher expertise

⇨ Conceptual methods: reading, analysis, hypotheses

Pragmatic

Core Qualities as Thinkers

- Practical, get the job done
- Resourceful, improvising
- Ask what needs to be done
- On-the-spot action
- Always ready to help

Behavior with Others

- Like to create success
- Negotiate easily, easygoing
- Responsive, need freedom
- Friendly, open

Needs as Learners

- Real problems
- Hands-on experience
- Useful activities
- Team players
- Interesting options
- Action methods:
  experiences, strategies

Personal

Core Qualities as Thinkers

- ♥ People and process
- ♥ Harmony, peace, connections
- ♥ Cooperation, ask who
- ♥ Conscientious for the cause
- ♥ Feelings with personal meaning

Behavior with Others

- ♥ Noncompetitive, caring, trusting
- ♥ Like to be appreciated
- ♥ Intense, idealistic, of the moment
- ♥ Cooperative, for the team

Needs as Learners

- ♥ Humanistic issues
- ♥ Collaborative learning
- ♥ Time to work things through
- ♥ Harmony
- ♥ Personal interpretation
- ♥ Process methods: groupwork, arts, music, writing

Divergent

Core Qualities as Thinkers

- Discovery, investigation
- Open-ended thinking
- Ask what if, what else, why not
- Experimentation, challenge, risk
- Get on with it, move on, escape

Behavior with Others

- Competitive, especially with self
- Questioning
- Independent, able to detach
- Enjoy and use conflict

Needs as Learners

- Excitement
- Fast-paced exploration
- Freedom of choice
- Useful conflict
- Original problem-solving
- Unconventional methods:
  open options, self-direction

Keep in mind that there are no right or wrong, good or bad learning styles. There are simply different ways of looking at and doing things. The most successful students learn to arrange schedules and assert themselves so they can learn in their most natural and effective style as often as possible. But when you can't have it your way, challenge yourself to stretch your limits and incorporate other style characteristics as well. (Learning styles expert Dr. Anthony Gregorc calls this "style flex-ability.")

When considering learning styles, remember these points:

◎ Everybody has a personal style.

◎ We all need to "style flex" from time to time.

◎ Every style has strengths.

Recommended Resource

Knowing how you learn best can help you make your life easier. What's your learning style? Find out with the help of this guidebook:

Learning Styles: Personal Exploration and Practical Applications: An Inquiry Guide for Students, by Kathleen A. Butler (Columbia, CT: The Learner's Dimension, 1995). Butler introduces the concept of learning styles and explains how you can determine your own learning style and use it to your advantage. Ages 12–18.

NoBody "Brown-Nosed" The Trouble I've Seen

> "The most important thing in acting is honesty.
> Once you've learned to fake that, you're in."
>
> **Sam Goldwyn**

So far, you may have been persuaded, among other things, to attend class, sit in the front row, and be sensitive to your learning style strengths. Now you're ready to begin refining your tactics.

Five Pointers to Living Apple-y Ever After

1. Always smile and at least pretend to be interested. One student interviewed for this book even received a public thank you as a result of his efforts in this direction: "There is one student in this class who makes teaching a reward for me. Each session he is all smiles, and it lifts my spirits." The teacher went on to thank the student by name.

Most teachers will never get around to publicly thanking you, but they do notice your behavior, and they do remember.

2. Ask only questions that your teachers can answer. (There are exceptions, but play the odds.) You can tell when teachers know what they are talking about. Ask your question then. Request that they amplify, explain more. Let them know you suffer from the same hunger.

THE TIME TO POSE YOUR INQUIRY IS WHEN YOU OBSERVE THE INSTRUCTOR BECOMING MORE ANIMATED, EYES BURNING WITH CRANIAL CRAVING, FISTS FLAILING THE PODIUM, THREE DOLLAR WORDS HURTLING TOWARD THE IONOSPHERE. OR MAYBE JUST A LITTLE BIT EXCITED.

3. Ask for information after class. Find out your teacher's classroom or office hours and discreetly pass by daily until you observe that he or she doesn't appear to be busy. Now is the time to strike, because the teacher is probably looking for something to do anyway. Pick your favorite discussion topic and ask where you can find more information. Be specific. Ask for appropriate journal articles, studies, etc. You don't actually have to read the material, but who knows, you might learn something.

Random Thoughts

For those cynics among you, who are not easily convinced, there is a lesson to be learned by watching reruns of *Leave It to Beaver.*

In one particular episode, Whitey and Beaver are raking Miss Landers's (their teacher's) yard. Whitey asks "The Beav" if he isn't worried about some of the guys thinking that they are trying to "butter up" Miss Landers. Beaver replies, "My father says it doesn't matter what other people think of you, only what you think of yourself."

And everyone knows, cliché or no cliché, Ward Cleaver was never wrong.

4. Keep in mind that some teachers have little or no sense of humor. Some even maintain that you can have a good time memorizing the Periodic Table of the Elements, reading the Preamble to the Constitution, or figuring out what "x" is. Don't try to amuse these people. Their lives have gone the way of vaudeville.

5. Always be supportive of other students in the class. Overly competitive, grade-mongering students who put others down in an attempt to elevate their own position are repugnant to most teachers. Compliment your classmates openly and often, but only when it is deserved. The teacher will be impressed by your generosity. One fringe benefit of a systematic approach to niceness is that sometimes it is contagious.

Teachers Are People, Too

Most teachers and professors, sooner or later, will reveal what their lousy childhoods were like and all that other David Copperfield kind of crap (even if they haven't read J. D. Salinger). These revelations provide a golden opportunity for you to enter the final transition from "gummer" to "gumshoe." "To paraphrase *Dragnet's* Sgt. Joe Friday, "It's your job. You're a student."

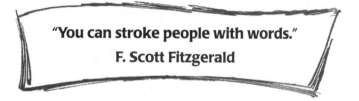

"**You can stroke people with words.**"
F. Scott Fitzgerald

You should take Sgt. Friday's advice. (Remember what happened to the lugheads and lamebrains who didn't?) Make your report card a decent place for grades to settle and raise your young average. And you may actually find yourself learning more than ever before in school.

How? Like any good detective, first, you should investigate, get the facts. Unfortunately, there will be times when you won't know what the facts mean. Teachers seem to delight in making references to obscure authors, unfamiliar events, and social causes that were unimportant even to their generation.

You must not allow yourself to become discouraged. Instead, you must dig to discover the background information necessary to apply these references in your course work and mediate your learning style with their teaching style. (After all, you can't expect *them* to change.)

To aid you in your beginning investigations, following is a sample Personality "Prof"-ile that a student might have compiled from a few weeks of careful listening in my class.

Personality "Prof"-ile

(The Inside Dope on That Dope McCutcheon)

Teaching Style

Evidence

- Except for the "Most Things in Life Should Be Organized Like a Bowling Team" speech, the lectures have been content-centered.
- Prefers debating ideas to general class discussion.
- Reinforces students who demonstrate use of logic and reasoning.

Conclusions

- Style could best be categorized as Analytical.
- Essays should be analytical as well as creative.
- Need original research to support theories— won't buy "seat of the pants" assertions.
- Must be willing to argue issues orally.
- Most receptive to making judgments based on a synthesis of available information.

Literature

Evidence (authors mentioned or quoted*)

-Poets: T. S. Eliot, Emily Dickinson, e e cummings, Lawrence Ferlinghetti, Dylan Thomas

-Playwrights: Harold Pinter, John Guare, Jules Feiffer

-Novelists: Max Shulman, J. D. Salinger, F. Scott Fitzgerald

Conclusions

-The guy either reads all the time or is one of those name-droppers.

-Tendencies toward dark comedy, abstraction, and romanticism dictate his reading habits.

-Using literary references in papers for his classes would be an effective strategy.

* If you haven't a clue as to who any of these literary types are, check out *Benét's Reader's Encyclopedia* or *Current Biography*.

Music

Evidence

-Singers/Songwriters: Bob Dylan, The Beatles, Simon & Garfunkel, Randy Newman.

Conclusions

-Symptoms of chronic "flower childness."

-Lyrics are important to him, so quoting songs would be effective in completing assignments.

-Sixties folk rock would be safest bet for consistent appeal.

Politics

Evidence

-Statements in class are apolitical but have slight liberal leaning. However, preferences in literature and music reveal stronger liberal commitment.

-His agreeing with the observation that democracy will never work because you can't have "wisdom through collective ignorance" is telling.

Conclusions

-Never risk a hard-line conservative position on any issue.

Sense of Humor

Evidence

-Laughs easily, sometimes when nothing funny is said or happening.

-Doesn't like crude humor. He was visibly upset at a student who told a sexist story.

-He never tells standard or formula jokes but seems to relish spontaneous puns or other types of creative word play.

Conclusions

-The more humor in assignments the better. (Restrictions: be original, be clean.)

-Most impressed by the "disassociated" ideas technique, so use whenever possible.

-Use of off-the-wall and dark comedy are appropriate.

The secret to a successful "Prof"-ile investigation is in the application of the gathered material in fulfilling homework and test obligations. The following examples illustrate how the information from a "Prof"-ile can be used in answering essay questions.

1. If you were taking a psychology class from me, you might be given the following assignment: Write a short theme on the topic "Couples break up as communication breaks down."

Before you commit a single word to paper, you study the "prof"-ile revelations and choose T. S. Eliot's "Love Song of J. Alfred Prufrock" for an introductory passage:

> **"Would it have been worth while . . .**
> **If one, settling a pillow by her head,**
> **Should say: 'That is not what I meant at all.**
> **That is not it, at all.'"**

Then, as you explain the communication gap that separates some couples, sprinkle in lines from Paul Simon's song, "The Dangling Conversation." Your conclusion returns to your original choice of T. S. Eliot, and you end with this final quoted passage:

> **"Till human voices wake us, and we drown."**

2. If you were taking a theology course, you might be given the following essay question on your final exam:

Is God dead?

Because you knew all along that this was a religion course, you have prepared by memorizing three generic approaches to any possible question on the subject. You have studied the "Prof"-ile, and you have chosen The Beatles' "Eleanor Rigby," Bob Dylan's "With God on Our Side," and "Sometime During Eternity," a poem by Lawrence Ferlinghetti. Again, you take the lines from one of these works and create a structural vehicle that specifically addresses the questions. (For imaginative ways to create these vehicles, see pages 56–63.)

Random Thoughts

Finding links between your particular "Prof"-ile and your actual course is not as difficult as it may seem at first. You must do some brain-storming and a little research, but big payoffs on grades are assured. Here are a few more examples to demonstrate that the ideas exist. You just have to find them.

> **Business**—The Beatles' "Taxman"
> **Sociology**—Paul Simon's "At the Zoo"
> **Art**—Ferlinghetti's "One of the paintings that would not die"
> **Political Science**—Randy Newman's "Political Science"
> **Math**—Adrian Mitchell's "The Accountant in His Bath" (clean humor)
> **Science**—Thomas Dolby's "She Blinded Me with Science" (off-the-wall lyrics)
> **Physical Education**—e e cummings's "nobody loses all the time"

Of course, the underlying assumption of this section is that all of your professors will have a personality. Let us pray.

All Work And No Wordplay

> "Imagination is more important than knowledge."
>
> **Albert Einstein**

Many years ago, a distressed teacher described her recurring nightmare to her colleagues. And although the details had long since faded from memory, the central image remained.

In this nightmare, the teacher found herself surrounded by hundreds of hands—no students, just their hands. Each hand grabbed at her, tugging at her, slowly dragging her down, until she collapsed.

Certainly, one of the rewards for teachers is the satisfaction of knowing that they have helped another human being to learn (leading a student to what legendary journalist David Brinkley observed in another context—"the dark at the end of the tunnel"). However, like our distressed teacher, *most* teachers believe they give much more than they receive.

The Empty Bucket Theory

The idea of constant giving has been referred to as the process of emptying one's bucket. The teacher dips into the bucket and quenches the students' thirst for knowledge. This raises the obvious question: Who refills the teacher's bucket?

The answer is simple. You should! And you should refill that bucket with cheap thrills. In creative and constructive ways, you should try to bring some entertainment into teachers' otherwise routine, academic lives.

Consider the following ideas as just a few of the possible empty bucket fillers. Then use your imagination and profit from the teacher's overflowing gratitude.

Variations on a Theme

Try to put yourself in the professor's shoes or, if you will, at his desk. In front of you is a pile of thirty essays, all on the same subject. Remember these essays are not written by Alexander Pope or Walt Whitman. These essays are best described as the "literary poop" of your dimwitted classmates. That's right, after this ordeal, the ol' bucket is going to be bone dry.

If you are a creative student, you will assess the open-mindedness of the instructor and change the assignment enough to make your paper different from the others. With luck, it may even be entertaining.

For example, there is an assignment that has now become a cliché in academic circles: the "What I Did Last Summer" essay. Imagine that you are given this assignment. You vary it and write "What I Did Next Summer." In essence, you are projecting yourself into the future but are using past tense in the treatment. The focal point of your work might be an analysis of last summer's mistakes as a basis for future decision making.

This unusual approach, still related to the basic expectations of the assignment, will make your paper memorable.

Parodies

A clever but often time-consuming effort is to write both what is required by the assignment *and* a parody of your attempt. Admittedly, this takes some thought, but the teacher will usually recognize and reward that extra effort.

Suppose that you are instructed to write a paper on the style of Ernest Hemingway, as reflected in the novel, *A Farewell to Arms*. You might also turn in the following parody of Hemingway's style.

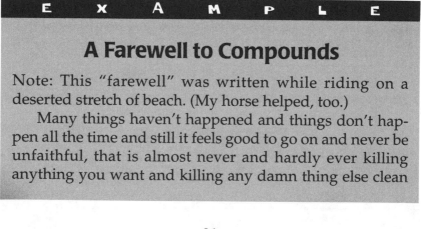

E X A M P L E

A Farewell to Compounds

Note: This "farewell" was written while riding on a deserted stretch of beach. (My horse helped, too.)

Many things haven't happened and things don't happen all the time and still it feels good to go on and never be unfaithful, that is almost never and hardly ever killing anything you want and killing any damn thing else clean and cleaning compound fractures of soldiers lonely in military compounds and after all, it was a hell of a war and so you write detached and unattached and unelated and usually unrelated . . .

And she was gone into darkness and more hardboiled nights and more romantic bastards searching and eating, drinking, and being merry welshing bottles full of hooch and autos full of girls very pretty and very modest and very wifely and Los Angeles was a very young city and we were very young and very, very and one and one was one and life was simple then and math was simple then and one and one was still one and compound love interest made two and in two nights death parted us for better and for worse and she returned far worse to dust and I returned to chemical compounds far better . . .

And you can stop your story the way you stop a life and you do not do it and afterwards you are not sorry and all of which and none of which has anything to do with glory and honor and courage and booting empty beer cans in Ketchum, Idaho, and the judgment comes and the compound sentence is served and sixty-two years turns into a life and then one day you run out of . . . "ands."

It should be pointed out that this parody was written without the benefit of having ever read a page of Mr. Hemingway's. The strategy, instead, was to read two short passages of literary criticism of his style and then exaggerate the described characteristics.

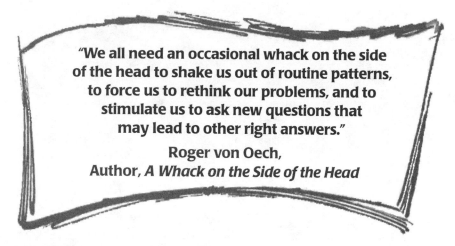

> "We all need an occasional whack on the side of the head to shake us out of routine patterns, to force us to rethink our problems, and to stimulate us to ask new questions that may lead to other right answers."
>
> Roger von Oech,
> Author, *A Whack on the Side of the Head*

Letters to the Editor

This seldom used avenue of expression has the potential to impress all of your teachers at once. The trick to writing a successful letter to a campus "rag" or local newspaper is to attack, in a satirical vein, some issue that you know will meet the approval of your average academician. You can always say nay to the niggardly nature of those nattering nabobs of negativism who refuse to pay your poor professors even a poverty level pittance. A letter guaranteed to make you popular. Or you could try variations of the following letter in which this "universal appeal" strategy has been used.

E X A M P L E

Dear Editor:

Early Monday evening as I was leaving Love Library, I was accosted by what was clearly a tubbed, grubbed, and freshly scrubbed freshman. Like most freshmen, he maintained the alert countenance of a recently gaffed salmon.

"Y'all know where the football stadium's at?" he twanged.

"It's that-a-way," I countered. He then countered up to 10 to prove that he could do it, and the conversation continued.

"Son," I began, "there is more to life than football."

He mulled over that morsel momentarily. "Yep! There's frat parties, too."

Being the glutton for punishment that I am, I pressed on. "But what about the Performing Arts Series at Kimball, the plays at Howell, the foreign films?"

Back to the old mullstream-of-consciousness. "Yep! There's frat parties, too."

Alas, I thought, it is time for more desperate measures. Fatherly advice.

"Son," I began again, "college is a lot like a football game. You chase a sheepskin instead of a pigskin, you gain knowledge instead of yardage, and you never violate the rules."

It was evident that my strained analogy was also straining him. So finally, to make a short story long and sensing the inevitability of his freshman fate, I resorted to realism.

"Son," I began again, again, "you need never despair that your education will interfere with football. The regents, state legislators, and other warm-hearted buffoons will never allow the University of Nebraska to become the 'Harvard of the Plains.' Their pride in the Cornhuskers is matched only by their pride in ignorance. (There is nothing quite as profoundly moving as the wheezing sigh of a freshman silhouetted against a magnificent Nebraska sunset.)

"In fact, you can write Mom tonight and tell her that now you have struggled through your first classes, you are one day closer to the opening kickoff of the 'Big Red Schoolhouse of the Astroturf.' "

Occasionally, you will need to make an excuse for an absence, a late paper, a low test grade. Be entertaining. Make even your excuses pleasantly memorable.

Val and Norman, two junior high school students, help us illustrate how this can be accomplished.

During class one day, Val wadded into a small ball the paper on which Norman had faithfully completed his math homework. Norman, although a tad irate, scribbled on the crumpled remains, "Val did this to my paper."

Val, observing this telltale message, and knowing the die was cast, created the perfect solution. Immediately, he wadded his own paper and penciled on his crumpled remains, "Norman did this to my paper."

There is a lesson here that should not escape you as you move on to higher education. In the world of excuses, it is best to be imaginative. In grade school it was acceptable to offer the flimsy ("My sister drew pictures all over my paper") or the improbable ("My dog ate it"). Now that you are older and must face teachers who are callous and inflexible, when forced to invent a rhyme or reason, try something confusingly clever: "I'm sorry about the late paper, sir, but my dog, rather artistically I might add, ate my sister."

THE THRILL OF THE HUNT

> **"Never learn to do anything: If you don't learn, you'll always find someone else to do it for you."**
>
> **Mark Twain**

Contrary to popular opinion, not all librarians are barbarians. Most of them are willing to help you, and you should cultivate their friendship. Indeed, they have the research keys to unlock the mysteries of most homework assignments.

All you have to do is learn to "borrow" the keys. Please consider these suggestions:

1. Act as if the librarians own the place. Pour on the compliments:

◎ Compare their magnificent library or media center to the pitiful one at your former school where you were frustrated for so many years.

◎ Show amazement at their skill in mastering this critical link in learning.

◎ Charmingly (and often) refer to your relative stupidity in these matters.

2. Avoid the Stanley Kowalski "I want it now" approach.* This seldom succeeds unless you notice the librarian chewing on the microfiche or relying on the kindness of strangers.

Fact Finding

Of course, manipulating librarians is just one method for gaining access to the library's "storehouse of knowledge." Here are some others:

* See the footnote on page 43.

◎ Phone former teachers who are both friendly with you and familiar with the library. (You'll be pleasantly surprised to find most are willing to assist.)

◎ Study with someone who is library-wise and doesn't mind showing off among the stacks. Former and current debate team members are usually good people to know.

◎ Hang around the reference books and ask someone who looks like he belongs there. Do not loiter by the *Reader's Guide to Periodical Literature* where every "dim bulb" goes. Be discriminating. Linger by the less trafficked areas—the *Index Medicus* or the *Index to the Book Reviews in the Humanities*.

◎ Make sure that you begin your research with a plan. Do not be like Stephen Leacock's famous horseman* and "ride off madly in all directions." You should think through all possible contingencies before they arrive or you will waste valuable time weeping on your *Webster's*.

◎ Being prepared with different approaches is imperative if you start your effort with information that is less than complete or is inaccurate. For instance, trying to find a Web site using a misspelled URL will get you nowhere (or it will get you to a number of sites you'd rather not see). You can imagine the potential confusion and wasted time caused by a typo on a handout or a teacher's scrawls on a blackboard.

◎ When organizing a subject search, keep in mind that in order to avoid catalog chaos, words or phrases known as "subject headings" have been chosen to stand for all their synonyms. The standardized subject terminology is based on the *Library of Congress Subject Headings (LCSH)*, more popularly known as the Red Books.

---

* Never heard of Kowalski or Leacock *or* his misguided horseman? Put this chapter's suggestions to the test and "LOOK IT UP!"

◎ A word of caution from one librarian: The Red Books do not include the most recently approved terms. You might be able to find entries in the library's online catalog under certain headings, but the headings could be too new to be in the Red Books. This means that you may still have to search the online catalog under related headings for newer terms, just in case they have not yet been included.

◎ If you are interested in members of the opposite inclination, then take this opportunity to really make your time well-spent in the library. Pick the most attractive member of the other sex to ask a question of. Take a chance on the laws of probability.

◎ If all else fails, teach yourself to use the library. Fortunately, there are books available to simplify this process. Here are some to try:

The Essential Researcher: A Complete, Up-to-Date, One Volume Sourcebook for Journalists, Writers, Students and Everyone Who Needs Facts Fast by Maureen Croteau and Wayne Worcester (New York: HarperCollins, 1993). Part encyclopedia, part almanac, part history book, *The Essential Researcher* is a handy reference for those who prefer to avoid the library whenever possible.

Find It Fast: How to Uncover Expert Information on Any Subject—In Print or Online by Robert I. Berkman (New York: HarperCollins, 1997). A how-to guide perfect for research novices or expert information sleuths, newly updated with a discussion of online research skills.

Finding Facts Fast by Alden Todd (Berkeley, CA: Ten Speed Press, 1992). This book teaches research techniques using libraries, directories, indexes, government archives, and periodicals. Learn the same methods that are used by reference librarians, scholars, investigative reporters, and detectives.

The Modern Researcher by Jacques Barzun and Henry F. Graff (San Diego, CA: Harcourt Brace College Publishers, 1998). Now in its sixth edition, this is a classic introduction to the techniques of research and effective writing and speaking.

Unweaving the Tangled Web

Along with contributing to the death of privacy, the Internet has given birth to a mega-info-mall. From banned books to basket weaving, you can connect to virtually any topic imaginable. For example, a pin drops in Timbuktu and there's an article about it on CNN Interactive. In the article, you'll find pictures, sounds, video clips, quotes from those who saw the pin drop, and links to related pin-dropping sites. And if the event you're researching is something major, chances are there's even a feature section on it that contains more information on pins dropping.

In fact, if you have an assignment pertaining to current events of any kind, check out CNN Interactive *(www.cnn.com)*.

One of the most useful things about CNN Interactive is that it's updated 24 hours a day, seven days a week. Let's say that you've just been assigned a paper on pins dropping in various locations. That night, you can get up-to-the-second info on the pin drop in question—so current that your paper is *much* more interesting and pertinent than your fellow students'.

Can't find what you're looking for at the CNN site? Then it's time to move on to a search engine. Many different brands of search engines are out there, but why try one when you can try them all? Go to Search.com *(www.search.com)*, the Grand Central Station of search engines, which allows you to board a multitude of engines and databases with a few clicks of your mouse button.

So what do you do with all the information you gather on your nighttime journeys through the Web? You can add the URLs where you found it to the "Bookmarks" or "Favorites" list in your Web browser, or you can save the information to disk and refer to it later. By no means should you simply copy and paste it into your paper and call it your own. To do so is plagiarism. Plagiarism is wrong. Don't do it. And don't succumb to those sites that encourage cheating.

Once you have an idea of what information is available to you, write an outline. With the outline in place, you then go back to the Web sites you bookmarked (or the disk where you saved the information), look up the facts you need, and add your own thoughts. Soon you're at the bottom of your outline, and your paper is finished.

Be sure that you format your bibliography or "works cited" page correctly for Internet papers, too. Because this technology is all a fairly new thing, most textbooks and guidebooks in schools don't explain how. Thankfully, the MLA Citation Guide is online at *atl46.atl.msu.edu/fall/citation.html*.

The Internet, however, is not a panacea for your brain pain. Consider some of the pitfalls of relying too heavily on the information highway:

- Anyone can publish on the Internet. The reliability and quality of information is often in question. Your gym teacher, for example, can dribble on and on and on in cyberspace—and you have no defense, no way to hand-check his credentials.

- Much of the good stuff you find lacks either context or historical perspective.

- You can get distracted by all of the useless junk that litters the information highway.

- The Web may cause you to overlook a more appropriate print source.

Therefore, don't confuse "easy to use" with "easy to learn." If you practice, though, you will become more proficient in finding what you need on the Internet. And you can have—to paraphrase reporter Joshua Quittner—your magic cookie and eat it, too.

Recommended Resources

Not quite Net-literate? Find help here:

Casting Your Net: A Student's Guide to Research on the Internet by H. Eric Branscomb (Needham Heights, MA: Allyn & Bacon, 1997). This book offers suggestions to make your time researching on the Net more efficient and productive—learn how to separate the good stuff from the garbage, find what you need fast, and give proper credit for the information you incorporate into your work.

The Internet for Dummies (4th Edition) by John R. Levine, Carole Baroudi, and Margaret Levine Young (Foster City, CA: IDG Books Worldwide, 1997). A practical, plain-English guide to what's new and necessary in the rapidly growing realm of the Internet and the World Wide Web. Be sure to keep it in your virtual glove compartment whenever you venture out onto the information superhighway.

NEW KID ON THE WRITER'S BLOCK

> "There is always a point in the writing of a piece when I sit in a room literally papered with false starts and cannot put one word after another and imagine that I have suffered a small stroke."
>
> **Joan Didion**

Writer's block is traditionally defined as an obstacle to free expression of ideas on paper, but any student who has once faced a writing assignment can tell you that blockage is a way of life.

Clearly, being forced to think is a pain in the brain. Having to write using that same process merely adds insult to injury. You become vulnerable. You listen to the doubts of your internal critics: "This paper is second-rate rubbish!" or "I couldn't write my way out of a paper bag."

You experience the dread that your external critics, both teachers and peers, will agree with your derogatory assessment.

You procrastinate.

You begin to do crazy things to avoid completing the assignment. Counting holes in ceiling tile, tapping out tunes with a #2 pencil, looking up dirty words in the dictionary.

IT DOESN'T HAVE TO BE THE MOON. JUST TAKE ME SOMEWHERE ELSE.

You sit down at the keyboard—

"The quick brown fox ..."

You sense the walls are slowly closing in. You open your mouth to scream, but there is absolute silence.

Each professional writer, like each student, confronts the reality of idea blockage. Oscar Wilde once claimed that he had spent the morning putting in a comma, and the afternoon taking it out again. F. Scott Fitzgerald found his solution in tap dancing. Beach Boy Brian Wilson placed his piano in a sandbox. A student I interviewed confessed that she formulated her best papers while sitting in the shower.

As you experiment with mind games (avoiding drugs and booze as options), I urge you to study the next sections carefully for concrete suggestions on how to stimulate creative juices.

Never Lose Interest in Borrowing

It was probably a hirsute graduate student, struggling to eke out an existence in some ancient academia, who, while playing "Mutton, Mutton, Who's Got the Mutton?" and idly carving a replica of his friend Ugg's new round invention into a nearby tree, first said:

COPYING ONE BOOK IS PLAGIARISM; COPYING SEVERAL IS RESEARCH.

No matter, really, who originated the notion, suffice it to say, the idea caught on.

In discussing plagiarism, it is important to draw some distinctions. Material considered in the public domain or "common knowledge" is traditionally (according to those in the scholarly community) handled differently than material protected by copyright. One who gives credit, of course, is not plagiarizing.

It is not surprising, then, that when writers give credit to others for "influencing" their work, it is many times merely polite writer talk for explaining away their wholesale borrowing.

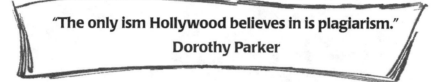

"The only ism Hollywood believes in is plagiarism."
Dorothy Parker

Most, but not all, authors will 'fess up to their filching. Woody Allen once readily admitted to borrowing from S. J. Perelman and Robert Benchley. Scholars are still debating the merits of Poe's savage attacks on Longfellow for aping European writers (and believe it or not, even the tender ballad, "Yes, We Have No Bananas" is strangely reminiscent of Handel's *Messiah*).

History is replete with alarming accusations of literary larceny.

Do not be shocked. All writers borrow from the past—their past experiences combined with their knowledge of literary or scientific or inventive works of the past. The successful ones do it more creatively.

The key to creative production of any sort is creative thinking—you must make the associations between the work of others and your experiences.

This important principle was made clear to this author when I was a high school journalist. My assignment on our paper was to crank out a biweekly editorial. In the first issue, after extensive research and soul-searching reflection, I strongly supported the thesis that my schoolmates should refrain from cutting into the lunch line.

This was coupled with a scathing indictment of shoving in the hallways. In short, I failed to break much new ground in high school editorial land.

I DON'T THINK YOU UNDERSTOOD MY EDITORIAL. I ONLY MEANT THAT I HAD A BURNING DESIRE TO READ...

By comparison, a contemporary of mine wrote an editorial that compared the future of the high school student to Shakespeare's "Seven Ages of Man."

Hmmmmmm . . . I thought.

In the paper's second issue, my editorial could have been condensed into the admonition, "Let's all be friends."

My contemporary, in his column, penned a eulogy to a local second-grade teacher who had recently passed away. The structure of the editorial was a time-capsule trip back to a typical day in this teacher's classroom. Without sentimentality, and with extraordinary sensitivity, the editorial paid tribute to how this teacher had changed her students' lives.

After reading and studying these editorials, it became painfully apparent to me that one of us was thinking creatively and the other was not. One of us was applying the principle of "borrowing" and the other was stacking marshmallows in the wind.

I learned from this literary lesson—I suggest you do the same. Begin by experimenting with the following formats that will add flair to any written assignment.

Literary Lessons

The Recipe Paper

The ingredients for this approach include passages from ten to twenty published sources, all related, in some way, to the subject of your essay. You simply lift a well-written group of sentences from each source and record this information on notecards. Then paraphrase (rewriting with as much imagination as possible) each notecard's contents on to a new notecard. Next, lay your cards on a table, read them aloud, over and over, until a common theme becomes evident. (Note: Not all cards will fit into any given theme. Be selective.) This common idea that you have discovered should be developed into a thesis statement (see page 63).

Now choose one of the most compelling cards. (This means that when you read it your reaction is, "Golly, that is amazing!") This statement becomes the introduction to your essay.

Finally, you place the remainder of the cards in their most logical sequence. Drop the irrelevant ones and group them into two or three major issues that explain or support the thesis.

All that's left for you to do is to write transitional statements linking the cards together and to add a finish to the paper.

The No Analysis Necessary Paper

This approach is used when you are required to write about a subject on which you have no previous knowledge. Or on a subject that is far too complicated for the limited time you have to complete the assignment.

Variation 1

A student taking an education class was asked to compare the ideas of Malcolm X to the "organic" teaching method of author Silvia Ashton-Warner. She decided to write an imaginary dialogue between Ms. Ashton-Warner and Malcolm X as if they were teacher and young student. No original thought was necessary because all of the lines were taken directly from published works by Ms. Ashton-Warner and Malcolm X (with proper credit, of course).

By simply matching lines from books, this student received an A+ on the paper. And she never had to directly address the complex challenge inherent in the assignment.

Variation 2

If you are asked to review a performance of a play like Samuel Beckett's *Waiting for Godot,* there is still hope.

A possible strategy in this case is not to review the play itself but the audience. During intermission and following the performance, carefully listen to the comments of audience members and record their mini-reviews. Some may even be willing to be interviewed more extensively after the performance or the next day by phone. Take all of your recorded responses and group them into categories.

Next, lift lines from the text of the play to use as introductory passages to those categories you've selected. For example, if you really did have to review *Waiting for Godot*, your three category headings might be based on the "anticipation," the "waiting," and the "disappointment." Just plug in the audience comments under the appropriate heading and write transitions.

Variation 3

For certain topics, the "Martian" approach may be effective. Let us say you were assigned to write a paper titled "Can the United Nations Ever Achieve World Peace?"

You write a first-person narrative as if you were a visitor from another planet. Naturally, you as an extraterrestrial and you as a student know nothing about international relations. How convenient for the both of you.

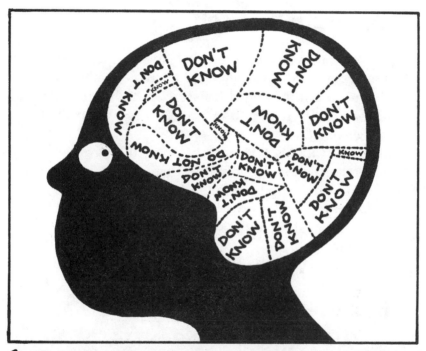

'MY, MY, THE THINGS THAT I DON'T KNOW WOULD FILL A BOOK!'

The Recycling Papers Gambit

If and when you finally write a first-rate paper, you should try to capitalize on your effort as often as possible. Try to persuade your teachers to allow you to shift their assigned topics to a topic that you have "always wanted to research." Or, if that doesn't work, ask if you can turn in a paper for extra credit; of course you forget to mention your paper was originally written for another class. (Some students I've talked to have essays that have seen more miles than Robert Frost, and more A's than *banana*.) Be sure to see if your school has any rules prohibiting recycling papers. If it is not permitted, take a pass on this option.

Paper Train Yourself

As pointed out in an earlier chapter, teachers are people, too. They have the same fervency for the frivolous, the same driving desire to bandy about boisterous badinage. After all, would you like to read and evaluate 30 essays on the lighter side of *Paradise Lost?*

Creative students take advantage of the weakness in the old academic armor. They clothe their content in structures that are tailor-made to tickle a teacher's fancy.

Following are descriptions of four more structural approaches that students have found successful. Admittedly, these creative vehicles may not, in themselves, change your life. But they do have the potential to change your grades.

1. Literary Droppings

It is often a wise strategy to let the teacher know you can read. And although using a literary device is not that original, it is almost always a safe choice.

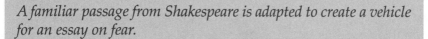

A familiar passage from Shakespeare is adapted to create a vehicle for an essay on fear.

> "All the world's a stage,
> And all the men and women merely players,
> And one man in his time plays many parts,
> His acts being seven ages."

These words from the pen of William Shakespeare, in his work *As You Like It*, remind us so vividly of the transience of life.

When Shakespeare wrote those famous lines, he could never have imagined how many of the players would someday suffer from stage fright. For them the stage—the world—is a fearful place.

W. H. Auden described this time in history as an "age of anxiety." Albert Camus called it the "century of fear." For indeed, according to the Health Institute of New York, some 18 million Americans are victims of irrational, persistent fears.

One out of every 12 of us is debilitated by these fears, and whether you realize it or not, the rest of us are adversely affected. Therefore, we must learn to control our fears, or most certainly, they will control us. Let us begin in the beginning.

"At first the infant, mewling and puking in the nurse's arms."

The psychologists' debate over an infant's "original" fears may never be settled. . . .

Katherine, 15

The play Sunday in the Park with George *is adapted to create a vehicle for an essay on self-determination.*

So Many Possibilities

"White. A blank page or canvas. The challenge: bring order to the whole. Through design, composition, balance, light and harmony." "So many possibilities." In these opening lines to the play *Sunday in the Park with George*, the character George Seurat envisioned an opening curtain rising, exposing an expanse of white, an expanse suggesting an untouched life, a blank canvas. And through design, composition, balance, and light, the painting would achieve harmony and become complete. And the images on that canvas would come alive and so would that untouched life. Like the artist Seurat, each of us chooses the brushstrokes that become a life. Unfortunately, as we are making choices, too many of us let other people control what goes on our canvases. We let others paint our lives away by allowing them to choose for us.

So, to begin our work of art, our lives, we must first take control of the design. And I believe that the design for our lives is limited only by the shape of our dreams.

Ladan, 17

2. Talk 'n' Role

The key to developing this vehicle is for the first-person narrator to assume a fictional role.

In writing a paper on the jury system in America, the narrator pretends to be a prosecutor placing that system on trial.

May it please the court. As prosecuting attorney in the case of *Justice v. the Jury System*, I am here today to prove to you, once and for all, that the jury system truly is an inadequate measure of justice.

Case in point: Pat Powis, a middle-aged San Francisco secretary, was asked to serve on jury duty in the Dan White murder case. She convinced the rest of the jurors that Dan White, who was seen killing the mayor of San Francisco, was not guilty. Pat's reasoning was that White, a former police chief, was unaware that murder was illegal.

Case in point: Edward Simpson, occupation unknown, was charged with rape in the case of *Simpson v. Utah*. After a six-month trial, he was found innocent because the jury failed to reach a unanimous verdict.

Eleven jurors voted "guilty," one voted "not guilty." As Mr. Simpson was leaving the courtroom, the one unyielding juror approached him and said, "We let you go this time, but don't do it again."

It seems the victim of this rape was raped twice: Once by Mr. Simpson, and once by our system of justice.

Implicit in these and hundreds of other examples is the belief that the jury system is not working. Ordinary citizens are simply not capable of or, in some instances, willing to do the job. Perhaps Herbert Spencer was right: "A jury is composed of twelve men of average ignorance."

We must all strive to make jurors both willing and able to serve jury duty. Until we do, it is time, ladies and gentlemen, for the jury system in America to go on trial.

Preeta, 16

In this passage, the narrator assumes the voice of comic-strip character Charlie Brown to discuss becoming an adult.

Good Grief

Good afternoon, my name is Charlie Brown. Many of you probably know me as the roundheaded bumbler in the "Peanuts" comic strip. I am sure that all of you know what it is like to lose, but I lost outrageously. I was a foul ball in the line drive of life, a missed field goal in the Super Bowl, 3 putts on the 18th green. I was a blockhead, a failure-face. But in spite of my failures, I've been around a long time. On October 2, 1980, "Peanuts" turned 30 years old. That same year, Mr. Schulz, the creator, had heart surgery and I asked him if it wasn't about time to let me grow up. Mr. Schulz decided to keep the comic strip the same, but to let me, Charlie, grow up in real life. Maybe his operation taught him how important it is to have a heart. Well, now that I'm in high school, I have found out that I can learn from all of my so-called mistakes. I know that the disappointments in my life, my failures, might actually make me a better person. In fact, I believe that every failure is trying to tell us something. We just have to listen.

Jason, 16

This narrator, in the tradition of Jonathan Swift and Mark Twain, has written a mock encomium, a form of satire in which pretended praise is actually blame. Incidentally, the paper from which this passage was taken received second place in the National Scholastic Writing Awards Contest.

I'm not crazy! I'm in touch with heaven. And it don't matter what you think 'cause I got a personal message from the Lord while watching Reverend Pat Robertson on the 700 Club. I was revelated through the Kingdom Principles and the word of knowledge. You know, I can still remember Rev. Robertson saying, "I have a word of knowledge." And he said, "There is a lady in Kansas City who has sinus. The Lord is drying up that sinus right now. Thank you Jesus. And there is a lady in Cincinnati with cancer of the lymph nodes. Well, I don't know if it's been diagnosed yet, but she hasn't been feelin' very well, But the Lord is dissolving the cancer right now. Thank you Jesus." And then, Rev. Robertson spoke right to me and he said, "My friends, there is a young lady in Lincoln, Nebraska, who can become a prophet for the Lord."

Sue, 16

More Ideas

◎ A paper written by Tom Sawyer set in the current year.

◎ An imaginary sequel to Sinclair Lewis's *Babbitt* in which Ted Babbitt (the son) discusses how his views on materialism changed during the Depression.

◎ A mock encomium treatment of military recruiting experiences.

3. Arts 'n' Crafty

These methods require throwing away your preconceived notions of essay form. The writing effort is usually more intellectually demanding and, thus, more time-consuming.

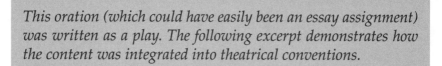

This oration (which could have easily been an essay assignment) was written as a play. The following excerpt demonstrates how the content was integrated into theatrical conventions.

The title of my oration is "It Is Greater to Be Human," a sadly human play about us. Our play is in three acts.

Act I
The curtain rises on the playground of life. Suddenly a child finds himself lifted from his mother's embrace and plopped into kindergarten, where each assignment is carefully graded, indicating to the child the exact amount of approval his performance has been awarded. His popularity with·teachers and students is contingent upon his degree of success.

"What did you learn in school today, dear little boy of mine? What did you learn in school today?"

"Our team's behind in the money race. Only four kids brought their money for the magazine subscriptions.

"My team won the baseball spelling game. I got three hits and one out. I misspelled goat."

Val, 17

In this passage, you will see how the idea of "making a difference in other people's lives" became an essay-turned-poem. This is perhaps the most challenging of approaches because so few young people, anymore, are versed in verses.

Take note that the student author has taken lines from e e cummings's work to introduce the reader to the poet's philosophy of life. Then, after the thesis statement (you, too, should make a difference), the author begins his version of cummings's famous poem, "anyone lived in a pretty how town." The final two lines illustrate how you can place original content in a borrowed structure.

It's no use trying to pretend that most people and ourselves are alike. You and I are human beings; most people are snobs. Take the matter of being born. What does being born mean to most people? Catastrophe unmitigated . . . you and I are not snobs. We can never be born enough. We are human beings for whom birth is a supremely welcome mystery. The mystery of growing, the mystery which happens only and whenever we are faithful to ourselves. You and I wear the dangerous looseness of doom and find it becoming. Life, for eternal us, is now. . . .

edward estlin cummings was never especially impressed by the heroics of the people convinced that they are about to change the world. He was more awed by the heroics of those who are willing to struggle to make one small difference after another.

In tribute to and in memory of Mr. cummings and anyone—I want to persuade you that you, too, should make a difference.

A Poem for Anyone
Anyone lived in a pretty condominium
with upstairs neighbors and privacy at a minium . . .

Craig, 17

63

4. Little Write Lies

This is a fun approach for the writer fortunate enough to have a teacher with an off-the-wall sense of humor. The idea is to begin your writing assignment with a lie. Then you cleverly shift to the true subject of your work. Incidentally, the following excerpt is from an essay that was used to win the National Championship in Original Oratory.

Boobus Americanus

Sunday, October 15. I am at the mall with a mission. No, not jeans, ice cream, CDs or cute boys. I am there to figure out the next four years of my academic life. Hundreds of booths are set up, each with an eager college representative passing out pamphlets, pinpointing information, and propagandizing anything pertaining to their school. It was the college fair, but fair it wasn't. Some booths couldn't attract a single soul. Being the clueless person that I am, I must have picked up a hundred pamphlets. It was at the end of my trek, though, when away from the mainstream I noticed *the* booth. Crowded with so many teens that I initially thought *Must be a party school*. I had to see for myself. Fighting through mobs of teenage girls and their mothers, I squinted to make out the university's name, "CLINIQUE BONUS TIME." Not a renowned university, but a universally known cosmetics line.

Instead of learning about, say, the University of Michigan application process, the girls had chosen to learn about the application of "Sheer Sable" blush. It shouldn't come as a surprise, then, that media researcher Jean Kilbourne tells us the Number One wish for girls ages eleven to seventeen is to be . . . on their high school speech team. You think I'm joking, don't you? Actually, what they really want has nothing to do with matters academic. They just want to be thinner. And, naturally, the Number One wish for boys is to have a girlfriend who's well informed. . . . Did I say well informed? What I meant to say is well formed.

According to author Steve Allen, Americans are suffering from a mental incapacitation, and he's not just talking about teenage boys and girls. To be blunt, too many of us have become what H. L. Mencken describes as the "Boobus Americanus," a bird too ignorant to know which way to fly. Well, ladies and gentlemen, it's time to wake up and fly right. Take a recent survey that revealed twelve-year-olds could name 5.2 alcoholic beverages, but only 4.8 presidents. A third of high school students did not know the U.S. had ever been involved in a war with Vietnam. Twenty-six percent of high school graduates could not identify Mexico on a map. And if you really want to be shocked I could share with you my SAT scores, but then I would begin to cry and my new Clinique mascara would start to run.

Reah, 17

Recommended Resources

Using funny, interesting, or just plain weird facts in your writing is an easy way to grab a reader's attention. You'll find many great ideas in these books:

The Book of Lists: The '90s Edition by David Wallechinsky and Amy Wallace (Boston: Little, Brown, 1993). Educational, revealing, and sometimes simply odd facts about famous people, places, and events. Great for adding spice to papers and speeches.

The Essential Researcher: A Complete, Up-to-Date, One Volume Sourcebook for Journalists, Writers, Students and Everyone Who Needs Facts Fast by Maureen Croteau and Wayne Worcester (New York: HarperCollins, 1993). Part encyclopedia, part almanac, part history book, *The Essential Researcher* is a handy reference for those who prefer to avoid the library whenever possible.

A Writer's Companion: A Handy Compendium of Useful but Hard-to-Find Information on History, Literature, Art, Science, Travel, Philosophy and Much More edited by Jerry Leath Mills and Louis D. Rubin (New York, NY: HarperCollins, 1997). From Ancient Gods to Rock Music, this reference contains everything a writer, editor, or researcher might ever need to look up, plus a whole lot more. It gathers a wealth of information not found in dictionaries, almanacs, or encyclopedias.

Quotations are a simple way to give almost any paper an extra punch. Each of these books is organized by topic:

The Penguin Dictionary of Twentieth-Century Quotations edited by J. M. Cohen and M. J. Cohen (New York: Penguin, 1996).

Peter's Quotations: Ideas for Our Time by Laurence J. Peter (New York: William Morrow & Co., 1993).

Simpson's Contemporary Quotations: The Most Notable Quotes from 1950 to the Present edited by James B. Simpson (New York: HarperCollins, 1997).

You Can Have Your Cake And Edit, Too

> "The language must be careful and must appear effortless. It must not sweat. It must suggest and be provocative at the same time."
>
> **Toni Morrison**

Research in language has revealed that English teachers prefer muddy, verbose writing to clear, simple writing. Syndicated columnist Charles McCabe summarized these new studies and pointed out that "Even people who can write good English prefer to write the pompous brand that so conned their teachers and continues to con their superiors and clients."

Therefore, we recommend two courses of action.

1. Spend an evening of heavy page petting and mental caressing with Strunk and White's *Elements of Style*. Make sure that the seeds of knowledge are firmly planted in your mind. This book is easy, particularly when compared to other forms of social intercourse.

Recommended Resource

The Elements of Style by William Strunk Jr. and E. B. White (Needham Heights, MA: Allyn & Bacon, 1995). The best book on this subject under 100 pages.

---

2. Add flair to the fundamentals by using "literary spicers."

◎ **Alliteration:** the repetition of consonants, especially at the beginning of words or stressed syllables. Examples:

—*Diversionary psychology, that marvelous new idea mesmerizing millions of Americans, that super new subject selling stacks and stacks of psychologically sensible suggestions in the blazing beauty of brilliantly bound books . . .*

—*The will to win is the combination of a work ethic plus the willingness to dedicate yourself to a worthwhile cause.*

◎ **Parallel Phrasing:** Repetition in structure; similar form and length in word choice. Examples:

—*If we accept the reality of our fears rather than avoiding them, and if we act realistically to face our fears rather than destructively to deny them, then and only then, we will be at peace when we reach retirement.*

—Lactogen is neither a disease nor a germ but a brand name. A heavily promoted and popular product in the third world, pushed as modernity at the loss of maternity, mortality, and morbidity at the loss of mother's milk. (In this example both alliteration and parallel phrasing are used.)

◎ **Similes and Metaphors:** A simile is an expressed comparison between two essentially different items, using a term such as "like" or "as." A metaphor includes a word which in ordinary usage signifies one kind of thing, quality, or action now applied to another, without expressed indication of a relation between them. A classic example of a simile is poet Robert Burns's

—"O my love's like a red, red rose."

However, we could change the line into a metaphor as follows:

—"O my love is a red, red rose."

Here is another metaphor as it might be expanded in an essay on greed:

—Little and big, our society is one of piggies. We are simply far too concerned with only ourselves. Most of us pass our days in isolated barnyards, wallowing in self-pity, dragging others through the mud, growing fatter until it just doesn't matter, snorting about this, sniveling about that . . . and never giving one generous "oink" for our neighbor pig.

◎ **Clever Wordplay:** Whether you're playing with puns or putting a new spin on an old saying, using clever wordplay in your writing adds interest for you and your reader. Examples:

—The thrill of popularity, the agony of not being neat.

—She sprawls on the couch, sagging skin slowly sinking into the vinyl, a 45 r.p.m. record left too long in the sun, a Salvador Dolly waiting for hello.

—Over prescription: When a hippocratic oaf prescribes too much of a drug.

—The subversive nature of the intellectual portion of our society also presents an enormous threat to our national well-being. With the sole exception of the Great Poultry Revolt of 1842 (known as the Chicken Coup), the eggheads have been the first to be jailed in any insurrection.

This example ties together Tennessee Williams's early plays with more recent pannings by the critics:

—With each new opening, a crass menagerie of critics urged Mr. Williams to take that one last ride on a streetcar named retire.

Clearly, the literary spicers provided in this section are just a sample of what can be done. Remember, though, very few of your classmates will make the effort to add these creative and compelling touches to their work. If you can sacrifice the time and endure the mental strain needed to spice up your papers, your work will increase in quality. Plus, many teachers will be so impressed by these flourishes that they will forgive some of the other weaknesses in your writings.

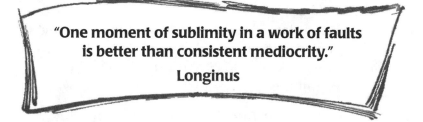

"One moment of sublimity in a work of faults is better than consistent mediocrity."
Longinus

Random Thoughts

Type or word process your papers. Handwritten papers with ruffled ridges and ink smudges to rival a Rorschach test are, in the age of computers, a surefire way to ruffle the feathers of even the most unflappable teacher.

If you can't type,

1. Learn, or

2. Barter with a non-creative student who needs ideas, or

3. Find someone who is willing to type for you.

Keep a backup copy of all of your papers.

1. Save your opus on disk (hard drives have been known to crash, and the old excuse "My computer ate it" probably won't fly), or

2. Make a photocopy. For a dime a page (average cost), you can avoid the heart- and brainache caused by the absent-minded professor who misplaces your Herculean effort and then claims you must have never turned it in. Just drop that copy on the desk and save the useless tears and idle threats.

Recommended Resources

Need more help with your editing? Check out these books:

The Deluxe Transitive Vampire: The Ultimate Handbook of Grammar for the Innocent, the Eager, and the Doomed by Karen Elizabeth Gordon (New York: Pantheon Books, 1993). A practical grammar book with a gothic twist, this style manual is fun to read and a great reference for those with a dark sense of humor.

Roget's International Thesaurus, edited by Peter M. Roget (New York: HarperCollins, 1994). This book can help you keep your writing fresh and interesting, even if you haven't had time to memorize your dictionary cover to cover.

Talking About People: A Guide to Fair and Accurate Language by Rosalie Maggio (Phoenix, AZ: Oryx Press, 1997). The author offers thousands of alternatives to outdated, stereotypical, offensive, and damaging language in this helpful handbook.

Woe Is I: The Grammarphobe's Guide to Better English in Plain English by Patricia T. O'Conner (New York: Putnam, 1996). A witty, jargon-free grammar and usage guide for those who don't know a gerund from a gerbil but would like to speak and write as though they did.

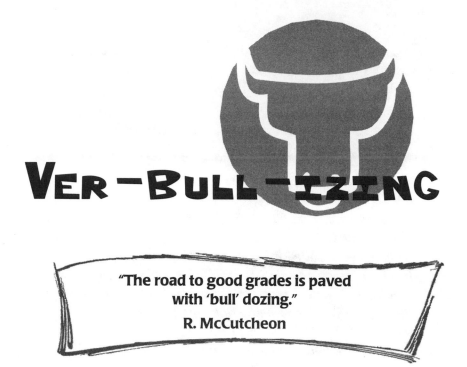

VER-BULL-IZING

> **"The road to good grades is paved with 'bull' dozing."**
>
> **R. McCutcheon**

In my checkered (but few checks) career as an actor, free-lance advertising copywriter, radio announcer, television movie reviewer, college and high school teacher, I have learned that the ability to communicate effectively is an invaluable skill for a lazy person—or, as my grandfather would say: "Yep, I was in the Battle of Bull Run. I shot the bull and it's still running."

Sadly for you speech purists out there, my grandfather had a firm grasp on rhetorical reality. The hallowed halls of the honor roll are crowded with students who have discovered this principle of sound over substance. A principle that means "It's not what you say but how you say it that matters."

Demosthenes, an oratorical oldie but goodie, was once asked what was the most important canon of rhetoric. He replied, "Delivery." To a second inquiry, he replied, "Delivery." And when asked a third time he answered, "Delivery." Well, you get the idea.

Politicians have fashioned careers around this self-evident truth. A classic example of how this process works is included in *The Book of Lists #2* by David Wallechinsky, Irving Wallace, Amy Wallace and Sylvia Wallace:

Claude Pepper v. George Smathers
U.S. Senatorial Primary Election (1950)

At the start of the McCarthy era, Floridian Claude Pepper, one of the Senate's most outspoken liberals, was on the conservative's "hit list" along with many other senators. George Smathers lashed out with some typical right-wing invective—he called his opponent "The Red Pepper"—and he launched a campaign to expose Pepper's secret "vices." Smathers disclosed that Pepper was a known "extrovert," his sister was a "thespian," and his brother a "practicing homo-sapien." Also, when Pepper went to college, he actually "matriculated." Worst of all, he "practiced celibacy" before marriage. Naturally, rural voters were horrified, and Pepper lost.

'MY MEALY-MOUTHED OPPONENT IS A WELL-KNOWN MASTICATOR!'

From this black day in campaign history, it is clear that Mr. Pepper, like the "Doctor" of the same name, was misunderstood. It should also be apparent by now, even to the uninitiated, that students who are skilled in speech have a distinct advantage over their silent partners in class. If oral discussions are counted as a factor in grading, then that advantage takes on increased importance.

I highly recommend that you force yourself to speak during class discussions. Do not argue that it doesn't make that much difference, that you don't know what to say, or that you are afraid to talk. Those are excuses, not valid arguments. If it's any consolation, here's what students have to say about speaking up in class:

> **"I always think, 'How stupid am I going to be if I ask this question?' But you have to ask or you suffer."**
> **Karlen, 18**

> **"Just think, you might be helping someone else out by asking your question."** Matt, 17

You must learn to speak in front of others if you want to make full measure of your potential. Denying the reality of your plight is futile rationalization. The point is moot, or should we say, mute.

Suggestions for the Scared Speechless

Here are some tips for overcoming the fear of ver-bull-izing:

- ◎ Ignore the advice to imagine the audience sitting out there in nothing but their underwear. This solution loses all psychological persuasiveness within a few seconds after what could have only been a disgusting mental picture.

- ◎ Forget the advice about staring at the foreheads or over the heads of the audience (or out the window or at a wall). A speaker's avoidance of direct eye contact becomes disconcerting to listeners, even if they're not sure why. Not looking people in the eye may be comforting to the speaker, but audience members are left feeling strangely uneasy. Instead, experiment with the following two techniques. They have been used with great success by speech students even when under the pressure of interscholastic competition.

1. Grin like a monkey. For most people, smiling confidently and being nervous are incompatible physiological responses. With the exception of those few who giggle and turn silly in anxiety, this approach of smiling when confronting the symptoms of fear is immediately calming. The trick is to force yourself to smile the instant you recognize the symptoms.

I'LL GRIN BUT I REFUSE TO BARE ANYTHING.

2. Make "instant jokes." The split-second you are aware of your anxiety, you should say a one-liner *(to yourself)*. Then quickly refocus your attention on the subject of your speech. Here are some examples:

—You feel drops of sweat pouring from your armpits and staining your shirt. You instantly say to yourself, "Great! I

won't need to take a bath this week." Immediately after, you return your full attention to the content of your speech.

—You are certain that your heart is pounding so loudly that people in the back row are quaking from the vibrations. Using the same basic process as before, you say to yourself, "Hooray, maybe someone will finally ask me to dance."

—Your voice cracks and you say to yourself, "Wow, at last I am passing through puberty."

In each case, the important step is to shift your concentration back to the speech right after you have made your "instant joke."

These techniques are designed to ease you through those periods of oral panic. They will not, however, help you in knowing what to say. Clearly it is impossible (and probably not desirable) for me to put words in your mouth.

Each class will demand different techniques. Each student comes with a different background. As a rule, however, if you are timid about talking in class, you should begin with some simple statements or questions:

❓ "May I get a drink of water?"

❓ "Would you please repeat what you just said?"

❓ "Is a nod as good as a wink to a blind horse?"

Or you might heed more serious guidelines when deciding when and what to ask of your teacher: If you can offer a constructive opinion, provide some new information, or support the discussion of a classmate, then you can be certain your observation is appropriate.

Now, I realize it is extremely difficult for some students to overcome natural shyness. Often, a reluctance to speak up in class is rooted in the fear of being thought of as "weird" or "looking like a fool."

To overcome this difficulty, try these two strategies:

1. Summarize and tie together the unrelated points your classmates have been making. This makes it easier for you to generate relevant discussion and get answers to questions that will fill holes in everyone's gaps of information.

2. Prepare a few questions the night before class and practice saying them over and over. You might take inspiration from the "airy persiflage" of my heroes Rocky and Bullwinkle.

The key to building confidence in your ability to speak in class is to start listening carefully to what other students say. Remember the 3 Rs of effective discussion. Your comments should be *relevant, reliable,* and *respectful.* (At the same time, you should avoid being *redundant.*)

Students who wish to reap the benefits of having more fun in class and better grades through ver-bull-izing will progress to whole paragraphs of public speaking. And from there to contributing serious content to class discussions.

Remember, for the lazy student, talk is cheap. But silence is oh-so-costly.

Recommended Resource

The Complete Idiot's Guide to Speaking in Public with Confidence by Laurie E. Rozakis (Topanga, CA: AlphaBooks, 1996). This guide helps you build the skills you need to deliver winning speeches and presentations. Offers solid information about how to communicate effectively with an audience for maximum impact; tips, definitions, and warnings to help you along the way; and clear illustrations that show you exactly what to do.

1. a (b) c d
2. a b (c) d
3. a b (c) d
4. (a) b c d
5. a b c (d)
6. (a) c d

THIS IS ONLY
A TEST

> "Do you happen to know how many tassels a Restoration Coxcomb wore at the knee? Or the kind of chafing dish a bunch of Skidmore girls would have used in a dormitory revel in 1911? Or the exact method of quarrying peat out of a bog at the time of the Irish Corn laws? In fact, do you know anything at all that nobody else knows or, for that matter, gives a damn about?"
>
> **S. J. Perelman**

In freshman English, my professor would refer to us collectively as those "happy hicks from huskerland" or "those "*#!!@* rubes from the farm," which seemed all right at the time, since we shared the same corny sense of humor. Between epithets of encouragement, however, he did make one observation that I have found to be a valuable insight into successful test-taking: "It's not how much you know that counts, but how well you use what you do know."

If you want to be "in the know," especially at test-taking times, consider the following:

1. Take comfort that you are not alone in the world of "temporary test trauma." Consider these examples of "lazy" students:

◎ *Thomas A. Edison, U.S. Inventor.* Edison's peculiar inquisitiveness as a young child impressed nobody but his tolerant mother. His first teacher described him as "addled," his father almost convinced him he was a "dunce," and his headmasters warned that he "would never make a success of anything." Under his mother's tutelage, however, Edison became a precocious reader, and he was soon making practical inventions. He eventually patented over a thousand inventions whose worth to humankind is incalculable.

◎ *Giacomo Puccini, Italian Opera Composer.* The creator of *Tosca, La Bohème,* and *Madame Butterfly* was born into a family of church musicians and was expected to follow the tradition. However, he was utterly unambitious. He did poorly in school and even caused his first music teacher to give up in despair, concluding that he had no talent. Happily, the approach of his second music teacher caught his fancy, and from that moment Puccini energetically devoted himself to music.

2. Fortunately for you, few tests require that you do much thinking. Despite continuing efforts to reform testing procedures, few changes have been made in the classroom. It is not surprising, then, that the Educational Testing Service concluded that the ways materials are taught in classrooms haven't progressed much in 25 years either.

What this means for you is that your achievement is still measured by your ability to memorize massive amounts of largely irrelevant information. Therefore, if you choose to make the best of a bad situation, refine your cramming techniques.

Initially, you need to be very selective about what you try to remember. Force yourself to choose only the most important elements that were covered in class. Drill on those items. If you attempt to memorize all of the material, your brain will probably malfunction from overload. Take a gamble on your judgment and drill, drill, drill. Recite aloud the important elements over and over and over and over and over again. Make use of mnemonic devices such as these offered by students in an advanced chemistry class:

- Leo says Ger (i.e., Loss of electrons is oxidation. Gain of electrons is reduction.)

- Roy G. Biv (i.e., the colors of the spectrum: Red, orange, yellow, green, blue, indigo and violet)

- Remember the story of "SOH-CAH-TOA"?

$$Sin = \frac{Opposite\ side}{Hypotenuse}$$

$$Cos = \frac{Adjacent\ side}{Hypotenuse}$$

$$Tan = \frac{Opposite\ side}{Adjacent\ side}$$

If you are conscientious in your drilling, then you will benefit from the "Vaccination Theory of Education." Neil Postman and Charles Weingartner, authors of *Teaching As a Subversive Activity*, used this theory to explain how once students have taken a course and passed the test, they are "immune" and will never again have to demonstrate any real learning in that subject.

3. Most teachers talk at a rate of about 100 words per minute. Believe it or not, you are able to think about four times that fast. Use that "extra" time to make sense of what is being said. Do that and you will significantly reduce the need for long hours of studying later.

4. Richard P. Gallagher, an educational consultant in Pennsylvania, recommends that you take notes only on the right-hand half of your notebook pages. Save the other half for your own comments and questions. Mr. Gallagher is on to something. Teachers are constantly giving clues to potential test questions by repeating a fact several times, by writing it on the board, or by subtly saying it will be on an upcoming exam.

5. When you are reviewing for a test, be sure to take a lot of breaks. After an hour or two of studying, people reach a point of diminishing returns. Pushing beyond your natural limits will not increase learning; it will merely decrease desire. The quality of study time is the critical factor in being adequately prepared. Therefore, study the most difficult subjects first, while you are most alert.

6. Pay attention to directions. On short-answer and essay questions, it is imperative that you figure out precisely what the question is asking. The exact wording of what is asked should dictate your answer. Key words in the questions will guide you. There is a difference, for example, between the verbs "compare" and "contrast." To "enumerate" is not to "analyze." However, the ambiguous "discuss" can be interpreted to mean "compare," "contrast," "enumerate," "analyze," "explain," "defend," "describe," etc.

7. Write neatly, be brief, and be clear. (Pencil is a pain to read, according to most teachers, so always use a pen.) Grading short answer and essay questions can be largely a subjective exercise. Don't give a burned-out teacher a reason to take out frustrations on you.

8. Do not form a "study group" unless you plan to study. Otherwise, you end up with a social group that gets together to avoid the loneliness of *not* learning.

9. Pick up a copy of *Acing College: A Professor Tells Students How to Beat the System* **by Joshua Halberstam, Ph.D.**

(New York: Penguin, 1991). The book is entertaining and honest. Halberstam begins by admitting that most professors are poor teachers. His subsequent advice is invaluable both to high school and college students.

10. In each class, always attempt to find old tests that were given by the same teacher. Most teachers are ambitious enough to continually create new questions, but there will always be patterns that you can decipher. For example, in true-false questions, does your teacher consistently favor one over the other? In multiple choice, does your teacher favor particular letters or use sentence patterns that are giveaways?

Closely examine not only the type of essay questions that the teacher asks, but also how this instructor evaluates the answers. Is more value given to content or form? How does the teacher react to creative approaches? Can you expect "trick" questions?

In short, studying old tests might be the most efficient use of your midnight oil.

11. In times of quiet desperation, when you suddenly realize that you are facing a major exam and you have no idea how to prepare, pay a visit to the teacher. You would be surprised how much valuable information can be acquired if you are both direct and tactful.

One student I interviewed demonstrated the good that can come of such a visit. He was dismayed to discover that his semester grade in Introduction to Political Science would be determined by only two hour-long exams and a final. Following a D+ on the first exam and a B- on the second, dismay turned into despair. At the last moment, reason triumphed over reluctance, and he set up an appointment with the professor.

The conversation went something like this: "I've always been an A student. But in your class, I've been disappointed with myself. I've worked very hard (expecting lightning to strike) but evidently in vain.

"I don't want any special favors . . . I'm willing to do all the work, but could you give me some ideas on what to study for the final?"

YOU MAY NOT BELIEVE THIS, BUT I AM WORRIED ABOUT MY GRADE...

The professor then handed him a sheet of paper that contained a list of ten questions. She informed him that the three questions on the final would be taken from the list.

Twelve hours later, the student had memorized ten compelling arguments with specific supporting material for each question. Fortunately, he didn't blank out the next morning. He scored an A+ on the final and received an A in the course.

It is important to note that not all teachers will help in this way. Not all would have given the benefit of the doubt when it came to final grades. But what if this student, for fear of rejection, hadn't asked?

12. When answering essay test questions, you will have greater success if you follow a specific structural approach. Here is a complete example from one student to give you a model to follow. Each section is annotated with an explanation of the necessary elements.

Q: How can we curb violent juvenile crime?

Recently, the *Washington Post* ran an editorial cartoon depicting one of the many problems facing politicians and parents alike as they attempt to reduce juvenile crime rates. The caption read, "The 'Get Tough on Crime' frenzy reaches an obvious climax. . . ." We see a woman still in the delivery room after having given birth to a baby boy. Two police officers are with them in the room. One is aiming his pistol at the baby exclaiming, "God knows what he's capable of!" His partner anxiously waits with an infant-sized prison.

This cartoon illustrates all too well how Americans are tempted to combat the growing number of criminals who are nowhere near having grown up. Children who should be hitting the books are finding themselves booked in juvenile detention centers, and middle-schoolers are committing murder. John Calhoun, former director of the National Crime Prevention Council, calculated that in 1994, males aged 14 to 24 made up less than eight percent of the nation's population, but committed over forty-eight percent of the nation's murders.

Such disproportionate numbers force us to ask ourselves the question, "How can we curb juvenile crime?" The answer to this question is that a balancing of prevention and punishment would offer Americans better alternatives to putting the baby before the carriage.

There are two methods of prevention that are most feasible. First, if children are supervised during those afternoon hours before their parents are home with them, they are significantly less likely to

[handwritten margin notes:]
← Creative intro into subject of essay. Cartoon adds to attention-getting approach.

› Use of imagery to link children to criminals.

← Quote an expert to stress importance of the issue.

› Transition into a precise statement of the question.

← Divide essay into two areas of analysis.

← Subdivide each area into two related points.

← First sentence of first issue.

commit crimes. A recent Connecticut study found that the majority of crimes committed by juveniles took place between the hours of 3 P.M. and 8 P.M. Criminologist at Northeastern University James Fox agrees, "We will see a significant drop in the rate of crime between 3 and 8 P.M. if we reorder the school day." With this in mind, President Clinton has supported legislators' efforts to provide supervision during those hours of the day by federally funding afterschool programs. Acording to the *Christian Science Monitor*, funding would be used to establish 1,000 new programs designed to occupy children during after-school hours.

Use of published sources add weight to your argument.

The second method of prevention targets America's parents. Lawmakers need to recognize the link between child abuse and juvenile crime. Those children who were neglected by the system seem more prone to lash out against it. *Newsweek* magazine recently estimated that sixty percent of boys arrested for violent crimes have a reported history of abuse and neglect. Even more startling, ninety percent of girls arrested for violent crimes reported having been sexually or physically abused. While there is no proof of causation, the statistics raise concern as we try to curb this national crisis. It is important when considering our safety from violent teens to also consider their safety from us.

First sentence of the second point.

Prevention is not the only possible tool for curbing juvenile crime. We also need to examine the options for punishment for those who do not respond to prevention. These options are twofold. One option is to treat young violent offenders differently than juveniles guilty

Transition into the first point of the second area of analysis.

of misdemeanors. Our court system needs to make the distinction between a juvenile vandal and a juvenile murderer, and stop seeing them as a collection of juvenile offenders. As the *Washington Times* reported, President Clinton has laid the foundation for such a distinction by allocating $50 million to establish special courts geared specifically toward punishing violent juvenile offenders.

The second and most frequently discussed option is to try juvenile offenders as adults. Theoretically, the nature of the crime should supersede the age of the criminal. Some states, with support from the federal government, hope to institute such systems, and their wishes may soon be granted. The *New York Times* explained that the House of Representatives has passed legislation sending $1.5 billion in block grants to states that try juveniles as adults. It seems that many state and federal politicians are recognizing what already may be obvious. As John Corbett, a judge in Plymouth, Massachusetts, noted, "If somebody does something wrong, there should appear to be some sort of consequence."

So, in the final analysis, when asking ourselves the question, "How can we curb juvenile crime?" we have seen that while the police officers in the cartoon may have been overreacting, they were headed in the right direction. A combination of prevention and punishment is the most viable solution. To neglect juvenile crime today is to set the precondition for an increase in those crimes committed by juveniles and adults alike tomorrow. For, as Jean Baptiste Racine once said, "Small crimes always precede great ones."

← *Second point of second issue.*

← *"Magic" transition to end can be used as summary link for any essay question. Simple sentence makes it seem question received in-depth answer.*

← *Reference again to thesis. (always repeat in conclusion)*

← *Impressive last sentences or "zingers" and their positive effect on your essay should not be underestimated. Teachers have a tendency, as we all do, to remember what they read last.*

Now that you have finished studying this annotated example, here is a sample examination question to test your mettle, as well as your mental abilities:

A man is walking down a road at four miles per hour. Another man is perfectly motionless but is holding five apples and four oranges. If gravity equals seriousness, and "x" is the 24th letter of the alphabet, then how much wood can a woodchuck chuck?*

Recommended Resources

Why study harder when you can study smarter? Learn how with help from these sanity savers:

"Ace" Any Test by Ron Fry (Franklin Lakes, NJ: Career Press, 1996). A practical guide to help you prepare better and study more effectively.

Last Minute Study Tips by Ron Fry (Franklin Lakes, NJ: Career Press, 1996). This useful book describes studying and test-taking methods for those dreaded last days, hours, or (too often) minutes before exam time.

* If you failed to answer, "As much wood as a woodchuck could chuck if a woodchuck could chuck wood," then you are easily distracted by extraneous information. I suggest you reread this chapter.

CUTTING COSTS THE McCUTCHEON WAY

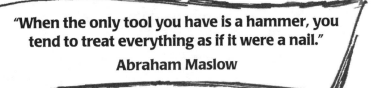

"When the only tool you have is a hammer, you tend to treat everything as if it were a nail."

Abraham Maslow

With the rapidly escalating costs of a college education, many students need to find ways to cut corners in their financial planning. Here are a few suggestions for reducing expenditures:*

◎ Sell your old tests—charge the price of photocopying plus what the market will allow (keep all originals to be sold again the next semester). Timing is critical in selling old exams; the closer the date of doom, the higher the price. Remind your customers of the penalties for essay question plagiarism and require them to sign a contract

---

* Use these ideas at your own risk!

guaranteeing ethical practices. Make them sign or don't sell. At all costs, be certain that the buyer has only the honorable intention of purchasing a study aid. And, of course, be aware of your school's policy on selling tests. Breaking the rules and getting suspended or expelled would take care of your college costs, too, but that's probably not exactly the type of solution you had in mind.

◎ Don't buy books that are in the library. Go to the bookstore a few days early, find out the required texts, and then, in collaboration with a classmate, take turns checking the books out of the library so that they never revisit the shelves. Don't forget that city libraries will often have some of the books, too.

◎ Read assignments in the bookstore. As a junior in college, I purchased none of the books that were required for my courses. Instead, I would stand, as inconspicuously as possible, and peruse the reading assignments right there in the aisles. I don't recommend this for everyone, but it is possible.

IT'S SO HARD TO FIND A BOOKSTORE AISLE WITH A VIEW.

Time Rarely Flies

A high school principal once advised me that upon entering the "real world" I should spend eight minutes on each personal appointment. His theory was that any less than eight minutes and the person I was meeting with would feel slighted. Any more than eight minutes would only mean that nothing else would be accomplished. I then intimated that class periods be scheduled to last eight minutes. I was unceremoniously chastised for missing the point.

Which brings us to the point of this chapter. . . .

When budgeting your time, the more selfish you are, the happier you are. But remember that in your attempts to be selfish, you will eventually fall prey to procrastination. This is an understandable behavior pattern when confronted by what W. S. Javons characterized as the "irksomeness" of work.

EVEN COWS GET THE BLAHS

However, there are techniques that you can try to over-come procrastination paralysis. These are just a few strategies recommended by Robert D. Rutherford, author of *Just In Time:*

1. Divide and conquer. Take what seems to be an insurmountable task and divide it into more workable parts. Writing a book of 300 pages can seem an overwhelming task. But if you divide the work into manageable parts and write 400 carefully chosen words a day, you'll have yourself a book in just six months. This concept, applied to the limited nature of daily assignments, will make them seem much less formidable.

2. Start with a part that is believable. If you are reluctant to do something because it is too large to take on, seems too difficult, or because you feel you cannot do it, select a part of the activity that you think is possible to complete. The old momentum theory will carry you on to tackle the rest of the project.

3. Make it ridiculous. If the task is tedious or seemingly unrewarding, exaggerate the completion of the project in a way that is laughable. For example, can you imagine your teacher waiting breathlessly for the assignment with a wheelbarrow full of $1,000 bills upon its completion?

4. Reward yourself big. Choose a part of a task that you have been putting off. Make the reward for completing that part so great (or the penalty so severe) that you have no other option than to do the task. A typical reward might be sleeping in an hour or two when you'd normally force yourself to rise and shine.

5. David and Goliath it. With this technique you simply face the problem squarely. There are going to be really tough assignments you just don't want to do. These are easily delayed. Nevertheless, they must be done. So—David and Goliath them. See yourself as battling an unpleasant, obnoxious, and obstinate giant. By defeating your imagined giant, you will feel the triumphant vibrations of victory. Or maybe just slingshot whiplash. (But it's worth a try anyway.)

6. Finally, in preparing to portion your life away, first schedule in a few hours to do nothing. Next, a few hours of planned recreation. This will make facing the rest of the day almost tolerable. A sample schedule from one lazy student's college days should help you understand this approach. (Please note that although this "typical" day is directed at male readers, the many insights into time management could easily apply to female readers.)

Tuesday

8:00 a.m. *Awaken to the joyous sounds of birds gargling and your roommate chirping. Arrgghh! You think. Still in the sleepy middle of a mental muddle, you succumb to sweet slumber.*

8:30 a.m. *Awake anew. You lie in bed pondering the difficulty of actually waking a gnu. Your mind wanders to memories of last night, the drive-in movie, "Mud Wrestlers from Outer Space versus the Mexican Mole Women" with Kinky Rodriquez and Gunther Montez, the familiar back seat of your faithful '57 Chevy and, of course, Betty Lou. Suddenly, you realize that those are someone else's memories . . .*

8:45 a.m. *Crawl off to the shower on all threes. Your tennis elbow is still asleep.*

9:15 a.m. *Return from the shower to primp and preen. It's not a pretty picture.*

9:30 a.m. *This is your first scheduled time to do nothing. You do it very well.*

10:15 a.m. *Leave for class early so you can sit in the front row.*

10:30 a.m. *Sociology 1+1, "Marriage and the Family"—you ask the professor a meaningless question: "How can a single woman like you teach a course about marriage?" You don't listen to her response but instead, dream of lunch . . .*

11:20 a.m. *Follow the most beautiful girl in class to where she chows down. You chew on the social significance of ambience at a restaurant like Wendy's as well as your cheeseburger.*

11:52 a.m. *Wipe your chin. Not from the burger, but the girl.*

12:00 p.m. "High Noon" break. If you are going to survive this academic pressure cooker, you must force yourself to relax once in a while. You do nothing for an hour. Very well. (Practice makes perfect!)

1:00 p.m. Study time.

1:15 p.m. Enough is enough! You go to class early.

1:30 p.m. Math Art 101, "Counting by Numbers." It occurs to you that Van Gogh was right, "Sometimes life just doesn't add up."

2:30 p.m. English 022, "The Beat Poets of San Francisco." You initiate a fake argument with a classmate as to whether these poets were really just Bongophiliacs who couldn't keep a beat or whether they should've been told to Beat It. You argue, quite persuasively, that they only wrote for the bread, man (the $). You lose.

3:30 p.m. Study time. You are a glutton for punishment.

4:30 p.m. Planned recreation. You watch reruns of "Leave It to Beaver," "I Love Lucy," and "The Andy Griffith Show."

6:00 p.m. Dinner in the dorm. You spend ninety minutes table-hopping from friend to friend so that you can fantasize about every female who reveals a healthy appetite.

7:30 p.m. Recovery from dinner. You lie down to allow the "Don't Be Gruel" soup and soybean surprise to settle. You chuckle to yourself that if dormitory dinners could be divorced, there would never be a just settlement.

8:00 p.m. Go to bed. Who are you kidding? You don't want to hit the books, you're not a hit with the ladies, and you're afraid you might hit your roommate, so you might as well hit the hay. After all, you're not getting any younger.

Recommended Resource

Get Organized by Ron Fry (Franklin Lakes, NJ: Career Press, 1996). Another great resource from study-tip/time-management expert Ron Fry, this book will help you study smarter.

Just In Time: Immediate Help for the Time-Pressured by Robert D. Rutherford (Boulder, CO: Keneric Publishing, 1998). Stressed-out as a result of too much procrastinating? Try this book's suggestions for improving your time-management skills.

And so it seems that our pages together have dwindled down to a precious few. If you have learned your lessons well, then you will:

◎ Attend class and sit in the front row.

◎ Analyze your strengths and weaknesses.

◎ Analyze your teachers' strengths and weaknesses.

◎ Struggle to become creative in your work.

◎ Use the many resources available in the library.

◎ Refine your test-taking techniques.

◎ Budget your time effectively.

In short, you will become a more successful student. You will still be lazy, but at least you will have the skills to survive the "massacre" of school.

Random Thoughts

We must all face the ravages of time, literally and figuratively. Philosophers have written volumes in search of an understanding of this idea of successive existence, infinite duration. However, my grandfather, a Nebraska farmer wizened by the inevitability of the changing seasons, had a penchant for separating the wheat from the chaff.

When asked, "What time is it?" my grandfather would invariably respond with a question, which was, in its own way, the answer that philosophers throughout the ages have failed to discover:

"Time all fools were dead; do you feel ill?"

Well . . . do you?

Index

A

"Ace" Any Test (Fry), 88
Acing College (Halberstam),
    82–83
Allen, Steve, vii, 65
Allen, Woody, 51
Alliteration, 68
Analytical learning style, 19
Arts 'n' crafty writing
    approach, 62–63
As You Like It (Shakespeare),
    57
Ashton, Warner, Silvia, 54
Attendance
    and boredom, 12–13
    and emotional trauma, 15
Auden, W. H., 57

B

Babbitt (Lewis), 61
Barzun, Jacques, 45
Beatles, 32, 33
Beckett, Samuel, 54
Benchley, Robert, 51
Berkman, Robert I., 44
The Book of Lists (Wallechin-
    sky and Wallace), 65
The Book of Lists #2 (Wal-
    lechinsky, et al.), 74
Bookstores, 90
Boredom, 5
    address for, 7
    strategies for, 9–15
Borrowing ideas, 50–53
Branscomb, H. Eric, 47
Brinkley, David, 34
Brown-nosing techniques,
    24–27
Burke, Edmund, 15
Butler, Kathleen, 17, 23

C

Camus, Albert, 57
Casting Your Net
    (Branscomb), 47
Classes
    choosing, 16
    skipping, 12–13
Cohen, J. M., 66
Cohen, M. J., 66
College costs, cutting, 89–90
The Complete Idiot's Guide to
    Speaking in Public with
    Confidence (Rozakis), 78
Conformity, 3
Copies of papers, 71
Cramming techniques, 80
Creative thinking, 51
Creativity, 5, 35, 36
Criticism, 48
Croteau, Maureen, 44, 66
cummings, e e, 33, 63

D

Decision-making, and learn-
    ing style, 17
The Deluxe Transitive
    Vampire (Gordon), 72
Demosthenes, 73
Didion, Joan, 48
Divergent learning style, 22
Dolby, Thomas, 33
Dylan, Bob, 32

E

Edison, Thomas A., 80
Editing, 67–72
    resources, 68, 72
Education
    college costs, cutting,
        89–90
    as deadly, 1–2
    timing of, vii
Educational Testing Service,
    80
Einstein, Albert, 34
The Elements of Style (Strunk
    and White), 67–68
Eliot, T. S., 32
Emotions, and attendance,
    15
Empty bucket theory, 35
Essays. See Writing
Essay tests, 84–87
The Essential Researcher
    (Croteau and
    Worcester), 44, 66
Excuses, 40
Eye contact, and speeches,
    75

F

Fake argument strategy, 11
Farewell to Arms (Heming-
    way), 36
Fear
    essay on, 57
    of failure, 5
Ferlinghetti, Lawrence, 32,
    33
Fili-blustering strategy, 11
Find It Fast (Berkman), 44
Finding Facts Fast (Todd), 44
First-person narrative, 58–61
Fitzgerald, F. Scott, 27, 50
Freud, Anna, 5
Friday, Joe, 27
Fry, Ron, 88, 96

G

Gallagher, Richard P., 82
Geography, knowledge of,
    vii–viii
George, Anthony, 23
Get Organized (Fry), 96
Giving, by teachers, 34–35
Goldwyn, Samuel, 24
Gordon, Karen Elizabeth, 72
Graff, Henry F., 45
Grammar resources, 72
Greenspon, Thomas, 2

H

Halberstam, Joshua, 82–83
Hemingway, Ernest, 36

I

Ideas, borrowing, 50–53
Imagination, 23
Index Medicus, 43
Index to the Book Reviews in the Humanities, 43
Internet, 45–46
  resources, 47
  See also Web sites
The Internet for Dummies (Levine, et al.), 47

J

Javons, W. S., 91
Jokes, and speeches, 76–77
Just In Time (Rutherford), 92, 96

L

Last Minute Study Tips (Fry), 88
Laziness
  defined, 2, 4
  reasons for, 3–4
LCSH. See Library of Congress Subject Headings (LCSH)
Learning styles, 16–23
  flexibility in, 23
  resources, 17, 23
  types, 17–22
Learning Styles (Butler), 23
Letters to the editor, 38–39
Levine, John R., 47
Lewis, Sinclair, 61
Libraries and librarians, 41–44
  as alternative to buying texts, 90
  resources for using, 44–45
Library of Congress Subject Headings (LCSH), 43–44
Lies, as writing approach, 64–65
Lincoln, Abraham, 8
Listening, as learning style, 16

Literary device writing approach, 56–58
Literary spicers, 68–70
Literature, teachers' preferences, 29
Longinus, 70

M

Maggio, Rosalie, 72
Martian writing approach, 55
Maslow, Abraham, 89
McCabe, Charles, 67
McCutcheon, R., 73, 101
Meaningless question strategy, 9–10
Memorization, 81
Metaphors, 69
Mills, Jerry Leath, 66
Mitchell, Adrian, 33
MLA Citation Guide, 46
Mnemonic devices, 81
The Modern Researcher (Barzun and Graff), 45
Morrison, Toni, 67
Moving, as learning style, 16
Music, teachers' preferences, 30

N

Narrative, first-person, 58–61
National Championship in Original Oratory, 64
National Scholastic Writing Awards Contest, 61
Newman, Randy, 33
No analysis necessary writing approach, 54–55
Note-taking, 12, 82

O

O'Conner, Patricia, 72
Oech, Roger von, 36
Opinions, by others, 26
Oration, 62, 73. *See also* Speeches

P

Papers. *See* Writing
Parallel phrasing, 68–69
Parker, Dorothy, 51
Parodies, 36–37
The Penguin Dictionary of Twentieth-Century Quotations (Cohen and Cohen), 66
Pepper, Claude, 74
Perelman, S. J., 51, 79
Perfectionism, 3
Personal learning style, 21
Personality
  "Prof"-ile, 28–31
  of teachers, 16, 27–33
Peter, Laurence J., 66
Peter's Quotations (Peter), 66
Plagiarism, 46, 50–51
Politicians, speeches by, 74
Politics, teachers' preferences, 30
Pope, Alexander, 35
Postman, Neil, 81
Pragmatic learning style, 20
Preferences, of teachers, 27–33
Procrastination, 48
Public speaking. *See* Speeches
Puccini, Giacomo, 80

Q

Questions, asking in/after class, 25–26
Quittner, Joshua, 46
Quotations, resources, 66

R

Reader's Guide to Periodical Literature, 43
Realistic learning style, 18
Recipe paper writing approach, 53
Recommended resources, 23, 47, 65–66, 68, 72, 78, 88, 96

Recycling papers writing
approach, 55–56
Research
Internet, 45–46
library, 50–53
resources, 44–45, 47
Roget, Peter M., 72
*Roget's International
Thesaurus* (Roget), 72
Rozakis, Laurie E., 78
Rubin, Louis D., 66
Rutherford, Robert D., 92, 96

S

Schultz, Charles M., 60
Seating location, and
boredom, 13–15
Seeing, as learning style, 16
Sense of humor, 26, 31
Seurat, George, 58
Shakespeare, William, 57
Shaw, George Bernard, vii
Shyness, and speeches,
77–78
Similes, 69
Simon, Paul, 32, 33
Simpson, James B., 66
*Simpson's Contemporary
Quotations* (Simpson),
66
Skipping class. *See* Classes
Smathers, George, 74
Smiling
in class, 24–25
and speeches, 76
Speeches, 73–78
overcoming fear of, 75–78
resource, 78
Strunk, William, 67
Studying
cramming, 80
old tests, 83
skills, 3

study groups, 82
time, 81
See also Tests and testing
Subject searching, 43
*Sunday in the Park with
George,* 58
Supportiveness, 26–27
Swift, Jonathan, 61

T

Talking About People
(Maggio), 72
Teachers
as giving, 34–35
personalities of, 16, 27–33
as resources, 43
teaching style, 28
and test ideas, 83–84
*Teaching As a Subversive
Activity* (Postman and
Weingartner), 81
Tests and testing, 79–88
directions, 82
essay tests, 84–87
old tests, selling, 89
old tests, studying, 83
resources, 88
reviewing for, 82
talking with teacher,
83–84
and teachers' notes, 12
test trauma, 80
testing procedures, 80–81
writing on, 82
Thomas, Dylan, 5
Thoreau, David Henry, 9
Thurber, James, 91
Time management, 91–97
example, 94–95
resources, 96
Todd, Alden, 44
Touching, as learning style,
16

Twain, Mark, 1, 51, 61
Typing papers, 71

V

Viewpoints (Butler), 17

W

Waiting for Godot (Beckett),
54
Wallace, Amy, 65, 74
Wallace, Irving, 74
Wallace, Sylvia, 74
Wallechinsky, David, 65, 74
Walpole, Horace, 13
Web sites, 43, 45. *See also*
Internet
Weingartner, Charles, 81
*A Whack on the Side of the
Head* (Oech), 36
White, E. B., 67
Whitman, Walt, 35
Wilde, Oscar, 49–50
Williams, Tennessee, 70
Wilson, Brian, 50
Woe Is I (O'Conner), 72
Worcester, Wayne, 44, 66
Word processing, 71
Wordplay, 69–70
Writer's block, 48–50
defined, 48
A Writer's Companion (Mills
and Rubin), 66
Writing
approaches, 35–39, 53–65
examples, 36–37, 38–39,
57–65
literary spicers, 68–70
resources, 65–66
style, 67–70
on tests, 82
See also Plagiarism

About the Author

Randall James McCutcheon was privileged to attend the college of his banker's choice. Although he subsequently graduated with distinction, his departmental advisor lamented, "If only Randy weren't so lazy, he would have wasted even more time studying."

In the years following graduation, he almost made a living as a graduate teaching assistant, advertising copywriter, radio announcer, and high school teacher.

Mr. McCutcheon was selected 1985 Teacher of the Year in Nebraska. He has received national recognition from the U.S. Dept. of Education and the National Association of Secondary School Principals for "innovation in education." He has taught in public and private schools in Nebraska, Iowa, Massachusetts, and New Mexico and has coached his speech teams to twenty-one state and five national championships.

A former student remembers, "Mr. McCutcheon talked real good for a coach. And loud, too."

The book, of course, speaks for itself.

Also by Randall McCutcheon:

Can You Find It? 25 Library Scavenger Hunts to Sharpen Your Research Skills (Minneapolis, MN: Free Spirit Publishing, 1991).

Communication Matters by McCutcheon, et al (Eagan, MN: West Publishing, 1993).

Other Great Books from Free Spirit

The Gifted Kids' Survival Guide
A Teen Handbook
Revised, Expanded, and Updated Edition
by Judy Galbraith, M.A., and Jim Delisle, Ph.D.
Our new and improved *Guide* brings together two best-selling Free Spirit classics, *The Gifted Kids' Survival Guide* and *The Gifted Kids' Survival Guide II*. Thoroughly revised, expanded, and updated, it features vital information on giftedness, IQ, school success, college planning, stress, perfectionism, and *much* more. For ages 11–18.
$15.95; 304 pp.; softcover; illus.; 7¼" x 9¼"

How Rude!
The Teenagers' Guide to Good Manners, Proper Behavior, and Not Grossing People Out
by Alex Packer, Ph.D.
Blends humor with solid advice about manners from A ("Applause") to Z ("Zits"). Hundreds of "Dear Alex" questions and answers cover everything from dating to skateboarding, table manners to thank-you notes, ethnic jokes to cliques. Learn how to be a host with the most (and a guest with the best), what to do (and not to do) when going online or waiting in line, how to act at the mall and the concert hall, how to make introductions, apply for jobs, and *much* more. For ages 13 & up.
$19.95; 480 pp.; softcover; illus.; 7¼" x 9"

Bringing Up Parents
The Teenager's Handbook
by Alex J. Packer, Ph.D.
Straight talk and specific suggestions on how teens can talk to their parents so parents will listen, and how to take the initiative to resolve conflicts with parents, improve family relationships, earn trust, accept responsibility, and help to create a happier, healthier home environment. For ages 13 & up.
$15.95; 272 pp.; softcover; illus.; 7¼" x 9¼"

Perfectionism
What's Bad About Being Too Good?
Revised and Updated Edition
by Miriam Adderholdt, Ph.D., and Jan Goldberg
This revised and updated edition includes new research and statistics on the causes and consequences of perfectionism, biographical sketches of famous perfectionists and risk takers, and resources for readers who want to know more. For ages 13 & up.
$12.95; 144 pp.; softcover; illus.; 6" x 9"

The Survival Guide for Teenagers with LD*
*(Learning Differences)
by Rhoda Cummings, Ed.D., and Gary Fisher, Ph.D.
Advice, information, and resources help teenagers with LD succeed at school and prepare for life as adults. Topics include LD programs, legal rights and responsibilities related to LD, jobs, dating, and making friends. Reading level tested at 6.2 (Grade 6, 2d Month). For ages 13 & up.
$12.95; 200 pp.; softcover; illus.; 6" x 9"

Fighting Invisible Tigers
A Stress Management Guide for Teens
Revised & Updated
by Earl Hipp
Proven, practical advice for teens on coping with stress, being assertive, building relationships, taking risks, making decisions, dealing with fears, and more. For ages 11 & up.
$10.95; 160 pp.; softcover; illus.; 6" x 9"

Making the Most of Today
Daily Readings for Young People on Self-Awareness, Creativity, & Self-Esteem
by Pamela Espeland and Rosemary Wallner
Quotes from figures including Eeyore, Maria Carey, and Dr. Martin Luther King Jr. guide you through a year of positive thinking, problem-solving, and practical lifeskills—the keys to making the most of every day. For ages 11 & up.
$10.95; 392 pp.; softcover; 4¼" x 6¼"

Making Every Day Count
Daily Readings for Young People on Solving Problems, Setting Goals, & Feeling Good About Yourself
by Pamela Espeland and Elizabeth Verdick
Each entry in this book of daily readings includes a thought-provoking quotation, a brief essay, and a positive "I"-statement that relates the entry to the reader's own life. For ages 11 & up.
$10.95; 392 pp.; softcover; 4¼" x 6¼"

To place an order or to request a free catalog of
SELF–HELP FOR KIDS® and SELF–HELP FOR TEENS® materials,
please write, call, email, or visit our Web site:

Free Spirit Publishing Inc.
217 Fifth Avenue North • Suite 200 • Minneapolis, MN 55401-1299
toll-free 800.735.7323 • local 612.338.2068 • fax 612.337.5050
help4kids@freespirit.com • www.freespirit.com

Visit us on the Web!

www.freespirit.com

Stop by anytime to find our Parents' Choice Approved catalog with fast, easy, secure 24-hour online ordering; "Ask Our Authors," where visitors ask questions—and authors give answers—on topics important to children, teens, parents, teachers, and others who care about kids; links to other Web sites we know and recommend; fun stuff for everyone, including quick tips and strategies from our books; and much more! Plus our site is completely searchable so you can find what you need in a hurry. Stop in and let us know what you think!

Just point and click!

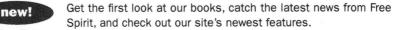

new! Get the first look at our books, catch the latest news from Free Spirit, and check out our site's newest features.

contact Do you have a question for us or for one of our authors? Send us an email. Whenever possible, you'll receive a response within 48 hours.

order! Order in confidence! Our secure server uses the most sophisticated online ordering technology available. And ordering online is just one of the ways to purchase our books: you can also order by phone, fax, or regular mail. No matter which method you choose, excellent service is our goal.

1.800.735.7323 • fax 612.337.5050 • help4kids@freespirit.com